KILLING JESUS

KILLING JESUS

The Unknown Conspiracy Behind
the World's Most Famous Execution

STEPHEN MANSFIELD
New York Times Best-selling Author

WORTHY
PUBLISHING

Copyright © 2013 by Stephen Mansfield

Published by Worthy Publishing, a division of Worthy Media, Inc., 134 Franklin Road, Suite 200, Brentwood, Tennessee 37027.

eBook available at worthypublishing.com

Audio distributed through Brilliance Audio; visit brillianceaudio.com

Library of Congress Control Number: 2013931705

Unless otherwise noted, Scripture quotations are taken from the *Holy Bible, New International Version®*, NIV®. Copyright © 1973, 1978, 1984, 2011 by Biblica, Inc.™ Used by permission of Zondervan. All rights reserved worldwide.

Scripture quotations marked NRSV are taken from the New Revised Standard Version Bible, copyright © 1989 the Division of Christian Education of the National Council of the Churches of Christ in the United States of America. Used by permission. All rights reserved.

Scripture quotations marked KJV are from the King James Version.

For foreign and subsidiary rights, contact Riggins International Rights Services, Inc., rigginsrights.com

ISBN: 978-1-61795-187-9 (hardcover with jacket)
ISBN: 978-1-61795-233-3 (international edition)

Cover Design: ST8MNT.com
Cover Image: Getty Images
Interior Typesetting: Susan Browne Design

Printed in the United States of America

13 14 15 16 17 LBM 8 7 6 5 4 3 2

To

Dr. Harold Paul and Dr. Jerry Horner

CONTENTS

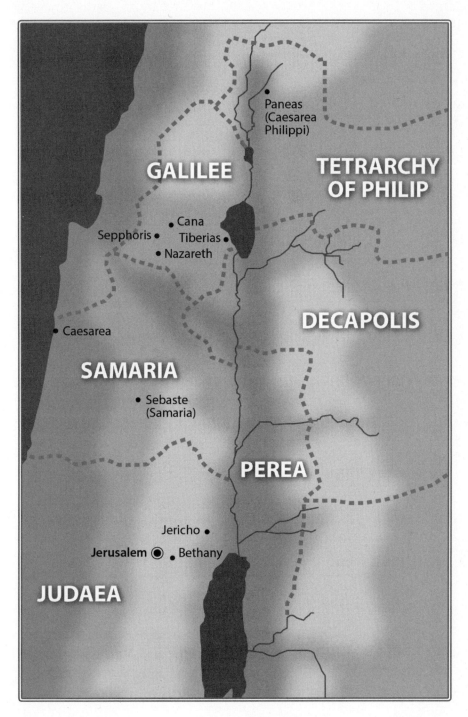

Israel in the Time of Jesus

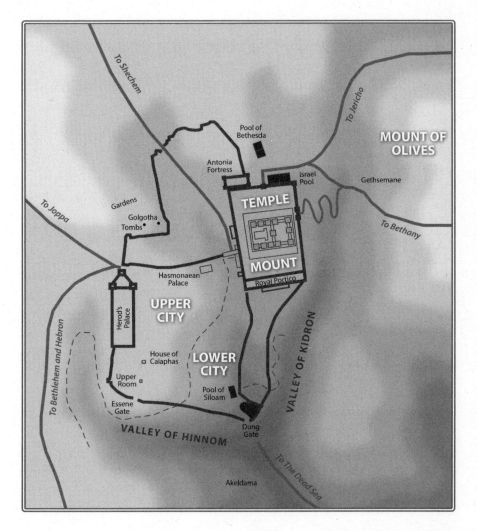

Jerusalem in the Time of Jesus

PROLOGUE

———

Jesus Christ was executed at a place so public that the sign explaining his death had to be printed in three languages, at a crossroads so well traveled that most of the people who saw him tortured were merely passing by. This is exactly what the Roman Empire intended: a demeaning, excruciating, public death the living would never forget. The revolting facts should not be obscured by a more pleasant tale. The stark, unsettling truth is that Jesus—impaled by Caesar's men—spent six hours gasping wide-eyed for breath while snarling, bitter crowds urged him to get on with the business of dying and soldiers ignored him to gamble for his clothes. It was savage, agonizing and exposed. Just as the empire intended.

The murder of Jesus, described in all its brutality and gore, stunned me when I first heard of it. I can remember the emotion on my professor's face as he recounted it in detail, how his words formed an image in my mind as though from a painter's brush. It stirred me, changed me. Even so, with the passing of years, I admit I allowed the image to fade. I could summon it in its lesser form as a religious duty, but the violent, nauseating version could not be made to stay.

Gratefully, that more haunting form returned to me as I wrote this book. This led to a crisis. The execution of Jesus began to live so vividly in my mind that it no longer seemed fitting to write about it in my cozy office of leather and brass. When I tried, I felt disrespectful, even defiant—as though I was smacking gum and checking e-mails at the funeral of a fallen soldier.

I had always written in cool, dim, quiet rooms, the outer world kept away. This was what I thought I needed to put words on the page. I started this book in just such a place. It didn't work. Try as I might to summon it, the story did not "live" in leathery isolation, would not reveal itself when I worked in self-important solitude. I gradually understood that this book was different. I could not seal myself off—ever the introvert, ever drawn to the lone and the quiet—and do justice to the sadistically public trial and torture of Jesus Christ. Realizing this, I knew what I had to do. I had to write about the killing of Jesus in the types of places where it occurred two millennia ago: in teeming, noisy, public places.

This is largely what I have done. Though I have completed the research where I had to—wherever scholars offered to meet me or essential volumes came to rest—I have written much of this work in the presence of distracted, hurried, uncaring crowds.

My desks were curbsides, park benches, lunch counters, café tables, subway seats, the concrete rims of city fountains, trash cans, car tops, and even parking meters. I have written at Hollywood premieres and in the middle of political protests, at National Football League training camps and at a packed restaurant with the man at the table next to me screaming something about dessert. Oddly, I wrote a paragraph or two within three feet of the Prime Minister of Israel. I wrote one urgent sentence in a crowded airport men's room: I thought the words might leave me if I waited. I even typed away bleary-eyed on a crammed, un-restful overnight flight from Tel Aviv, the dust of the Mount of Olives still on my shoes.

I arrived at most of these places in the natural course of my travels. There were some locations, though, I had to include no matter how far out of my way they were. For surely understandable reasons, I wanted to write some of this in a cemetery. The privilege of living in Washington, DC, allowed me to write at Arlington National Cemetery, but this came after I had already worked in an ancient hillside cemetery just beyond the walls of Jerusalem. Some of this story demanded to be written in the presence of armed men and imposing fortresses. The United States Pentagon, where I managed to write some lines before giving a speech, served quite well. So did the lunch table of an Israel Defense Forces (IDF) squad near the Citadel of David. To make the experience complete, I had to write in markets, courthouses, and cathedrals. I did. For this last need, Washington's National Cathedral, St. Anne's near Jerusalem's Lion's Gate, and the magnificent Christ Church Cathedral in Nashville, Tennessee, were gracious hosts.

In time, where I wrote became less important than the souls that surrounded me. I wanted to be where people rushed about, the burdens of the world upon their minds. I found no shortage of such places. An example is my beloved Union Station in Washington. I wrote there by the hour as though transported—the tribes of humanity rushing by and life-size statues of Rome's Praetorian Guard peering down. It was magnificent—and oppressive—just as Rome intended.

In all of this, I was not in search of inspiration. That came from the biblical accounts and from the theologians and historians I consulted. Instead, I was looking for gravity. To write of a bloody conspiracy surrounded only by books or the stifling silence of libraries is to risk sanitizing, floating above the human nastiness and carnage like a tourist in a foreign country trying not to soil his clothes. I didn't want to pass by unharmed, unmarked. I wanted to feel the threat. I wanted the bruising masses around me to grind me into the story's grit.

I find this essential to understanding Scripture. The Bible reveals sacred truth but it does so through a less sacred-seeming drama—an often earthy, troubling, lewd, starkly human drama. We are not meant to be embarrassed or rush quickly by. We are meant to know the story against the stormy age in which it happened—with all the grimy details fully in view—and to accept it as part of the way God speaks. Blood, spit, wine, semen, sweat, and the offscouring of generations spill out onto the page. No apologies are offered. This is the thrashing human drama of God, not some dainty pious tale. This is the Bible!

This is why the conspiracy to torture Jesus to death should not be read in too much of a hurry, with too much eagerness to get the body into the tomb—or beyond. There is meaning in every facet, revelation even in the daily and the mundane. We have not been given a ghostly myth that hovers among the clouds. We have been given the crass story of a political murder in a violent age, a murder committed after the guardians of virtue decided to kill a man because he was too much competition. There is more here than we usually see. There may even be more than we are willing to face. We should ponder every word, envisioning the story as fully as we can.

It is not a story best put on the page in an elegant library or office. It is better remembered where men and women curse their leaders while waiting for a train or where hardened souls scowl their way through threatening nights or where police officers help a bleeding, screaming man while uncaring diners sip expensive wines nearby. The execution of Jesus was a crime born of the streets, the barracks, the enclaves of the privileged, and the smoke-filled back rooms of religious and political power brokers. Its meaning lives in these places still. I am grateful I was forced out into that world to find it.

—*Stephen Mansfield*

A Brief Word About Violence

Working with my publisher and my amazing team of editors and advisors, which includes some of the finest scholars in the world, I have strained to be factual in this book, particularly in recounting episodes of violence. Never would I want to add to the stream of meaningless gore that fills so many of our generation's books and films. Still, it is not possible to describe the crucifixion of Jesus faithfully without including scenes of shocking cruelty and slaughter. The story itself demands this, but there has been no attempt here to exaggerate for effect. Torture, infanticide, brutality, murder, and even some subtle sexual themes appear in these pages, but only because they were part of the conspiracy to murder Jesus. The sensitive should beware, as should parents of younger children.

ON SCHOLARS AND SOURCES

The story of Jesus' death is simple enough to capture the heart of a child and yet vast enough to consume a scholar's life. It is like an epic poem that is movingly written and yet emerges from a genuine history. The art, of course, is to tell the tale in all its simplicity and force, while satisfying the demands of the facts.

This brings us to scholarship. The crucifixion of Jesus is so familiar as a tale of faith that it is easy to ignore the confirmation of it that comes from outside the Bible. We need this confirmation, if for no other reason, to move the story from the realm of faith alone to the certainties of time and place. It means we also need the work of dedicated scholars to help us know what we cannot know from the biblical accounts alone and to separate fact from persistent fiction. This seems particularly important in our current cynical age, when to merely suggest that Jesus actually existed can spark controversy. Neither the faithful nor the disbelieving should want this story floating mystically above us, unreachable. We want it woven into the fabric of first-century Jerusalem, genuine and textured, the smell of manure and sweat in the air. Scholars help us in this and we need their imprint upon these pages.

Still, we need to be careful. We do not want a narrative larded with academic tedium any more than we want a lightweight tale that ignores the counsel of experts.

A compromise, then. In the main body of this book, we let the story run its course, let it weave its meaning unrestrained. No debates. No intellectual turf to defend. We let the story work. When the tale is told, though, there follows a section filled with sources, justifications, explanations, and a bit of academic fire. Rejoice! Josephus will have his say. Tacitus and Pliny shall sound forth.

There shall, however, be no footnotes of the usual kind. This is a necessary act of academic rebellion, a vital stage in the author's recovery from sourcing abuse. Let us be done with little numbers stinging the eye and desecrating the text. It is time for such criminal intrusions to end. Instead, sources and commentary will be listed by page in the back of the book where other scholarly input also comes to rest.

CHRONOLOGY OF A CONSPIRACY

c. 6 BC	John, later known as "the Baptist," is born to an elderly couple somewhere near Jerusalem in the land of Israel.
	Six months later, Mary, wife of the carpenter Joseph, gives birth to a boy in Bethlehem. Rumors circulate that the child is illegitimate. He is given the Hebrew name "Yeshua," which the Greek-speaking world later pronounces as "Iesus." The name "Jesus" evolves thereafter.
4 BC	Hoping to kill Jesus, Herod the Great sends soldiers to Bethlehem to execute all male children under the age of two.
	Mary and Joseph hide their son in Egypt until they are sure Herod the Great is dead.
	King Herod the Great dies an agonizing death in the city of Jericho.
	Upon returning to Israel, Joseph and Mary learn that Herod Archelaus, son of Herod the Great, reigns in Judea. Fearing the hunt for their son continues, Joseph and Mary settle in Nazareth, a city in the northern region of Galilee.
6 AD	King Herod Archelaus dies. Herod Antipas, tetrarch of Galilee, takes his place.
25 AD	In the fifteenth year of Tiberius Caesar, John begins announcing the coming of the Messiah.

26 AD	Jesus is baptized by his cousin John, experiences forty days of temptation in the wilderness of Judea, and begins calling men to follow him.
	Jesus performs his first miracle at a wedding in Cana.
27 AD	Jesus begins his public ministry. Among his first acts is driving merchants from the Court of the Gentiles at the temple in Jerusalem.
	Jesus speaks at the synagogue in Nazareth, his hometown. The audience becomes so enraged over his statements about Gentiles that they try to murder him by throwing him from a cliff.
	Pharisees and teachers of the law discuss charging Jesus with blasphemy. In Israel, it is a capital offense.
28 AD	After Jesus heals a man on the Sabbath in a Galilean synagogue, Pharisees and Herodians conspire to kill Jesus.
	Teachers of the law from Jerusalem publicly accuse Jesus of being demon possessed.
	Herod Antipas, tetrarch of Galilee and Perea, has John the Baptist beheaded.
	On several occasions, Jesus declares publicly that there is a conspiracy to murder him.
29 AD	Religious leaders in Jerusalem strategize to kill Jesus. He ministers mainly in Galilee to avoid capture.
	Pharisees warn Jesus that Herod Antipas plans to assassinate him.
	In winter, while Jesus is speaking in the temple, a crowd attempts to stone him. He escapes and leaves Jerusalem for a season.

30 AD	In Bethany, Jesus raises his friend Lazarus from the dead. Religious leaders in nearby Jerusalem hunt for both men to slay them.

In a meeting at the house of Caiaphas, the reigning high priest, members of the Sanhedrin renew their commitment to assassinate Jesus.

9th of Nisan: Jesus enters Jerusalem from the east on the first day of the Feast of Unleavened Bread. He uses symbols—like choosing to ride a colt that had not been ridden before—to identify himself as a king. On this same day, Pontius Pilate, Prefect of Judea, enters Jerusalem from the west at the head of hundreds of Roman soldiers.

10th of Nisan: Jesus drives moneychangers and their customers out of the Court of the Gentiles in the temple.

11th of Nisan: While standing on the Mount of Olives, Jesus once again predicts the destruction of Jerusalem.

12th of Nisan: Two days before Passover and the Feast of Unleavened Bread, chief priests and scribes search for opportunity to arrest Jesus and put him to death.

- Judas Iscariot approaches the chief priests of Israel and offers to betray Jesus.

13th of Nisan: Jesus instructs his followers to prepare a Passover meal to be eaten later that evening.

14th of Nisan: After a Passover meal with his followers, Jesus is arrested by hundreds of Roman soldiers and temple guards in a garden surrounding an olive press on the Mount of Olives.

- Late that night, he is interrogated first by Annas (the former high priest), then by Caiaphas (Annas' son-in-law, the reigning high priest), and finally by most of the Sanhedrin. He is beaten, charged with blasphemy, and put in jail until early the next morning.

continued

30 AD	• Early the following morning, the Sanhedrin meets again to rule that Jesus is guilty of blasphemy and that he should be condemned to death. They take him to Pontius Pilate.

• Early the following morning, the Sanhedrin meets again to rule that Jesus is guilty of blasphemy and that he should be condemned to death. They take him to Pontius Pilate.

• Within an hour of the Sanhedrin's ruling, Jesus appears before Pilate at the Praetorium. Pilate questions him, sends him to Herod for interrogation, and—though Pilate believes Jesus is innocent—has him scourged. The crowd that has gathered at the Praetorium demands crucifixion. Pilate eventually acquiesces.

• *9:00 a.m.:* Jesus is taken to the place of execution called Golgotha, a small hill of rock just west of the city. Roman soldiers impale him upon two crossed beams.

• *3:00 p.m.:* Jesus dies. He is removed from the crossed beams and buried in a tomb owned by a member of the Jewish ruling council.

16th of Nisan: Friends of Jesus begin reporting that he has come back from the dead.

Inceptum:
THE BEGINNING

The Winter Palace
Jericho
March, 750 Years Since the Founding of Rome (A.U.C.)

The dying, seventy-year-old man ponders the apple and knife he holds in his hands. Though armies of servants tend his every wish, it is his custom to pare, cut, and eat his apples himself. He had intended to observe this custom now. Instead, the short, dull blade of his knife holds his attention. It whispers of possibilities he has never considered before, certainly not as gratefully as he considers them now.

He is dying and he is dying in inexpressible agony. It makes onlookers retch to see him. Doctors report that something like embers burn inside of him, a slow fire that actually emits a glow. This tortures him and at the same time it makes him ravenous, first for one type of food and then for another. Eating only adds to his torment. His inner organs are diseased and dissolving. A vile liquid oozes from his orifices and pools disgustingly at his feet. It secretes readily from an opening just beneath his belly. His penis is decaying and gangrenous. Worms fill his scrotum and push through the open sores that cover his genitalia. His body convulses constantly. There is no relief. When he sits up, he finds breathing difficult. When he lies down, he is nearly smothered by his maladies. His breath reeks of his decay. Doctors fear he is going mad.

These sufferings are what make him ponder the knife. To his diseased mind, it seems an escape. He looks eagerly about and, seeing no one near, he raises the tiny blade and plunges it swiftly toward his chest. Before it pierces flesh, a firm hand catches his arm in midair. It is the hand of his first cousin Archiabus, who holds fast and screams for help.

Others quickly appear, and the frail, dying man cannot resist them. He is held against his will. It is a rare moment for him, though, for he is the *basileus*, the king. In fact, by decree of the Roman Senate, he is the "King of the Jews." It is a grand title for one born "Hordos the Idumean." It seems even grander now that he is little more than a worm-ridden wretch. Still, until he breathes his last, he is the king—the one history will call Herod the Great. And he does not intend that any should forget.

He has dedicated his life to a bloody ascent to power. In doing so, he has ground underfoot much that was once dear to him. The Roman Senate declared him king and then gave him an army with which to capture Jerusalem. That was four decades ago. The Jews he was meant to rule despised him. Attempting to win their favor, he wed Mariamne, a member of the former Jewish royal family. When he later suspected her of complicity in a coup, he had her strangled and he murdered her sons. In all, he married ten times. It has proven dangerous to be Herod's wife.

During his four-decade reign, he has killed and killed often, murdering not only wives and sons but also his uncle, brother-in-law, mother-in-law, and even those he called friends. Hundreds more have died by his hand. He has ordered people killed by strangulation, assassination, burning, drowning, and cleaving in half.

There is more killing to come. Even in these last hours, while he putrefies and drains his life into the humiliating puddle at his feet, he orchestrates death. He already knows he will not be mourned when he dies. The thought haunts him. He has lived to be remembered. It is why he spent fortunes remaking Jerusalem into a city of the world. The temple, his palace, a variety of grand fortresses—he extravagantly constructed each so that he and his city would never be forgotten.

But he has shed too much blood, has lived too treacherously. He will not be grieved. Instead, his people will rejoice when he dies. He has simply visited too much suffering upon the land. Yet he, of all who live, knows how to make sure history does not forget.

Once again, he is planning murder. He has issued an order commanding the ruling men of the nation to assemble in the hippodrome. After they gather, he will have them executed. He will do this not because they have done anything deserving of death. Rather, he wants someone to mourn for something, anything, on the day he dies. He knows there will be no weeping for him. But he can at least make sure there are tears! He can—once again— cause sorrow and pain.

While this slaughter nears, he also plans vengeance upon his own flesh and blood. His time is short. He is settling accounts. He believes his son Antipater has betrayed him. He sent a message to Rome asking Caesar Augustus for permission to execute the traitor. Herod wants to kill his own eldest child. Disgusted, Augustus refused to get involved. The King of the Jews needed nothing more. His soldiers murder Antipater and bury him in an unmarked Persian field. Augustus comments that it is safer to be Herod's pig than to be his son.

These, then, are the last days of Herod the Great. Poisons of mind and body contort him. Suicide seems an escape. For relief, he plans bloodshed. He is determined to be remembered—even for evil, even for a legacy of anguish and sorrow.

Just before he breathes his last, ending the agony of his presence in this world, the foreigners come.

They are religious men, they claim, yet they seem more sorcerers or magicians than priests. They come from far to the East and practice some form of superstition that has them divining knowledge from the heavens. This is how they first saw the star. They claim it signals the birth of a king and so they have followed it. It stopped here. They hope for Herod's counsel. They yearn to worship the one so great that the heavens announce him.

They tell this first to Jerusalem's gatekeepers and then to the priests, who investigate, and finally to Herod, who had already heard the rumors crackling through the teeming city streets. He has already consulted the chief priests and teachers. He is already panicked.

That foreign magicians chase an errant star does not disturb him. What terrifies him is the phrase "born king of the Jews." This is what the easterners said. Their star leads to one born to be king. It is everything Herod fears, everything he has worked to prevent. He has murdered and schemed to stave off just such a possibility:

that a legitimate ruler might arise and take the nation from his family's hands, leaving him lost to history—unremembered and unmourned.

Bedridden and hemorrhaging, Herod summons the venom to plot death once more. Between the Jewish prophecy that the chosen one will be born in Bethlehem and the magicians' assurance that their star first appeared two years before, Herod knows who and what his enemy is. He need not be in a hurry. He can let these foreign priests do the hard work. He charms them. He feigns interest in their charts and their incantations. *Find this anointed one*, he urges. *We must all worship this new king*. The magicians leave with a commission to return soon and report what they see.

Herod waits. It is less than a morning's ride to Bethlehem. He expects the magician-priests to return the next evening, surely no later than the second day. Yet that second day comes, as do the third and the fourth, without any word. Weeks more go by and the king stops expecting. He knows he is betrayed.

The sadistic rage that has defined his life now concentrates upon a single human being. There is a "destined one" now living who would steal all he has built. The thought stings Herod's diseased mind. "Born king of the Jews." He feverishly turns the phrase over and over while he convulses on pus-soaked sheets.

Then, a certainty possesses him. *It must not happen. This Starred One must not live. No matter what is required, this man must die. Now. While this pretender is still an infant.*

Herod gives the order. *End the threat. Go to Bethlehem. Destroy all boys under two years old.*

His commanders make it so. Immediately. In the town with the name that means "House of Bread," where King David received his crown, soldiers snatch infants from their play and cut them in two. Some they stab while still in their mothers' arms. Others they behead. There are no more than three hundred people in Bethlehem, so there cannot be but a dozen boys under two years of age. The work is quick then, yet so ghastly that grieving mothers scream like wounded animals and do not stop for days. Some imagine the matriarch Rachel, whose tomb is in Bethlehem, weeping for her dismembered sons.

Herod dies believing he has killed his rival. At his last breath he is confident there is no other king of the Jews. The throne is secure for his descendants, his memory preserved for generations to come.

But it is not true. He failed to kill his rival. Whatever souls he snuffed out in Bethlehem, he did not slaughter the one who will one day claim to be Israel's true king. Nor did Herod secure his legacy. He married ten wives who together gave him fourteen children, yet a hundred years after his death not one of his descendants will be alive to perpetuate his name.

What he does leave is an unfinished mandate. There is an essential task he has left undone. How simple it is: there can be no chosen one. There can be no aspiring king who claims he comes from God. Rome will not put up with it. Nor will those who rule the temple. They have too much at stake. The fate of the whole nation depends upon completing this single task. If there is anyone, anywhere, saying God has destined him to rule, that he is the true king over Israel, then that man must be killed. There is no other choice.

This mandate embeds itself into the unspoken law of Jerusalem. The next time the opportunity presents itself, there can be no failure. This chosen one must die.

Piaculum:
THE SACRIFICE

The village of Bethany
Southeastern slope of the Mount of Olives
Two miles east of Jerusalem
Thirty years after the death of Herod the Great

The man the authorities plan to kill has just arrived. It has taken him six hours to walk the thirteen miles from Jericho, the city where Herod the Great died, where Herod's son Archelaus built an opulent palace, and where the Israelites first won victory upon entering the land of promise.

He might have been here sooner. He had intended to pass quickly through Jericho and to arrive in Bethany yesterday. Then crowds had formed and the road had filled up with people eager to watch as he passed by. This slowed him down, but it was that pitiful tax man who caused the big delay. When he saw the blustering little official sitting on the high branch of a tree, trying to see over the heads of his taller neighbors, something about the scene had moved him and he decided to spend the night in the man's house.

This disgusted the gossips and the narrow of heart, who thought it wrong for a man of God to associate with publicans—despicable men who collected inflated taxes to profit for themselves. They would sell their own people to Rome. Few are as hated. Yet that night changed everything in Zakkai's life. He stopped being a traitor to Israel and became a righteous man in the course of one evening.

The next morning, the hunted one pressed on. He was just putting Jericho behind him when a blind man called to him from the side of the road. There were appointments to keep, but something he heard in the voice calling out from its darkness captured him. He spoke with the man and with a second blind man who was there too. Then, without ceremony, he restored their sight. They wept and clung to him, the pain of the blackened years seeping away. He, knowing what the future held for Bar Timaeus and his companion, asked them to join him on the road to Jerusalem.

Finally, he has arrived in Bethany with his men. It is a strategic move. The authorities suspected he might sneak into the city during Passover to lead some kind of revolt. They put out the word that if anyone knew where Jesus was, he had a duty to inform. He has outwitted them. He has come six days before the Passover and has decided to stay just an hour's walk from the City, though on the opposite side of the Mount of Olives from Jerusalem. He is within reach but out of view, then, and the authorities cannot find him.

He has come here for yet another reason, something other than trying to stay alive. Bethany is where Lazarus lives, the man he raised from the dead a few days ago. When the temple officials heard about it, they decided once again they had to kill Jesus. They decided to kill Lazarus too. The authorities wish this story of resurrection to go away. Jesus has come to Bethany to make sure it does not happen.

It is Friday, the 8th of Nisan. This evening *Shabbat,* the Sabbath, begins. Friends are holding a feast in his honor, for Bethany is hailing him as a hero. It is being held in the home of the man called Simon the Leper—though he is a leper no more. Mary and Martha, grateful for their brother's return from the dead, excitedly serve the guests.

This is what he needs now: to relax among friends, to lean back against the cushions around the table and slowly, deliberately taste the food. He needs a cup or two of wine and a well-told story and some meaningful conversation with his men.

But then it happens. He is savoring the sumptuous meal. A small crowd of onlookers watches from the edge of the light. Suddenly, Mary steps behind him. She has a marble-looking bottle in her hands, and when she abruptly breaks it open, everyone recognizes the smell of nard. The discerning know by the scent that it is actually pure nard—and shockingly expensive. Without waiting for permission, she pours the silky perfume upon his feet. The guests stare in wonder. *Why hasn't she left this for the servants?*

Mary stops. Some are relieved, but then, she does the thing that ought not be done. Slowly, naturally, she reaches up and unbinds her hair. There are protests. She doesn't care. Her hair falls loosely about her shoulders, something a respectable woman would only let happen in private. Then, with utter calm, she takes a portion of her hair in her hand and uses it to rub the nard into his feet.

He does not move. He receives. A woman with her hair unbound is kneeling at his feet and rubbing appallingly expensive perfume upon him with her hair. It is understandable that some in the room should squirm. The nard is worth a year of a workman's wages, and yet it is being poured out on one man's feet? The news will spread. It will be a scandal. Then there is the matter of this woman and her familiar ways. Surely he knows what they will say about this. He should know, since he allowed this to happen once before, slightly more than two years ago when he first started out. A woman was involved then, too. His men remember the waste and the shame and the questions. For some it is far too much. They rage. *How dare she! The expense! The presumption!* They start pushing Mary away.

He raises his hand. This stops them. He seems moved and says he is grateful to her. She has prepared him for burial. *Take care of the poor whenever you want.* He says this to the ones incensed by the price of the perfume. *Take care of them well, for they will always be with you. But I'm not here much longer. Let her do what she was meant to do.*

After this, nothing is the same. His men look at him differently.

One of them, the one who tends the money and keeps the books, is so disgusted with this wasteful, sensual display that he slips out the back door. He knows what to do. The others are from the mountains up north but he's a Judean. He's local, has connections and understands the way things work. He leaves to make the necessary arrangements, certain the man he has been following is no longer a man of God.

Illegitimus:
THE ILLEGITIMATE

Judea and Galilee
Thirty years since the death of Herod the Great

The man the officials in Jerusalem are hunting sits in Simon's house in Bethany, smelling of nard and noticing the doubt in the eyes of his men. It does not trouble him. He has faced doubts about who he is his entire life.

Perhaps it helps that he is a Galilean. It has made him more rugged, more comfortable being alone, and maybe a bit less dependent on the opinions of other men. People can hear the difference in his voice. It has a unique character, but also that distinct accent. In fact, all the men who follow him, except for the ever-disgusted one named Judas, have that northern shape to their words. It marks them as outsiders down south in Jerusalem. And it doesn't help. The authorities dislike lowborn rubes from the hills as much as they dislike opinionated, nonconforming rabbis.

His name is *Yeshua*. He is called many things now but this was the name given him at birth, the name he grew up hearing when his parents called him or his friends wanted to play. Yeshua ben Joseph. Later on, this was how the people in town referred to Joseph's famous son. As his influence grew, the Greeks called him *Iesous*. In time, this would evolve into *Jesus* for much of the world.

In secret, some call him Mary's Bastard. His mother tried many times to explain. People were unwilling to hear. She became pregnant through unique circumstances. It was God who gave her the child, she insisted, though the folks in the village thought they'd heard otherwise. Joseph may have made everything right by choosing not to divorce Mary but it didn't change the facts. Jesus was someone else's son. Mary had been fortunate. She and Joseph were engaged at the time and when he learned of her pregnancy he could have put her away. The shame would have shadowed her the rest of her days. She might also have been executed. The law commanded death for adultery, and some still insisted upon it. Joseph saved her, but he couldn't save his son from living under the burden of suspicion and rumor. Yeshua ben Joseph of Nazareth: Mary's Bastard.

He knew who he was, but this made it no easier to live among those who didn't. His mother tried to help. She reminded him of the visitor's words and of what the old ones told her at the temple when he was forty days old. His father tried also, sometimes recounting the dream—the one that kept him from walking away and told him to make Yeshua his own. It touched him that his parents remembered these moments so tenderly. He certainly never forgot. Who he was never left his mind. It made perfect sense to him, for example, that he would stay behind and talk to the professors that time he traveled with his family to Passover in Jerusalem. He was only twelve but he knew what to do. He was safe the whole time and felt perfectly in place. His parents never fully understood. It was the difference between their calling and his.

He grew. He learned how to live among men. He also learned the ways of wood and stone from his father. They were close. When a man and his son work with their hands side by side, a bond forms. It can grow beyond the normal affection of fathers and sons to a masculine love that remakes casual friends into comrades, sons into trusted allies. But then Joseph died and Yeshua grieved as sons do and, as the oldest, cared for his mother from then on.

She was grateful for his devotion but she had other sons and daughters to look after her and Yeshua had a larger purpose. When he was almost thirty, she seemed frantic that it should begin. Perhaps she thought tending her had distracted him. Perhaps she needed some sign that the words from those many years ago were true. Whatever she felt, she pushed him, like a mother eagle pushing the eaglet from the nest.

It happened at that wedding just north of Nazareth, in the village of Cana. The celebration was winding down and the wine was running low, but no one expected more. Several had already consumed too much.

Mary told him about the wine like it was his problem to solve. It wasn't, though, and he told her so: *Woman, what is this to you and to me? It's just not my time yet.* In the way of mothers through the ages, she acted as though she had not heard and told the servants to do whatever he said. He hesitated, but this was, after all, his mother who was insisting. She had already endured much. Perhaps she needed this more than the guests needed wine. And she was staring at him. Expectantly. Hopefully.

So he did as she asked. The guests never forgot it. The best wine of the day and it came from six large jars of water when the feast was nearly over. The bridegroom and the bride were thrilled. The banquet master never knew exactly what happened but talked about the excellence of the wine all over town. His mother seemed—content. This is how it all began, with this first, forced miracle.

Then he simply did what he knew came next. He had already visited his second cousin Yochanan, who was baptizing people in the Jordan River. The stubborn wild man had to be talked into it, but he finally baptized his relative just as he had thousands of others. And that's when God spoke, though not all heard.

Forty days in the wilderness came just after. Forty days of pushing against the darkness. It felt like every temptation he had ever fought conspired together to ambush him. This time they came with a voice and seductive promises. Whole nations were promised to him if he would just give himself over to his enemy. Sometimes he could actually imagine giving in, but then he would pull back and see the offer for what it was. He fasted. He held the truth of scripture against the vanities that formed in his mind. He stared down the taunts and the lies. In time, the voice went silent and he was comforted. And power came.

So, it began. He did the astonishing things he was shown to do and taught the truths he had received. He became famous—and despised. He gathered a band of men to be at his side. They were clumsy but somehow comforting and they were devoted to him as far as they understood.

Always he knew that behind the crowds and the overly polite priests and the questions from the wealthy and the shrewd, there was something coming for him. He felt it before he saw it. He was being hunted by some kind of predator. It was nameless and faceless at first, but it was there. It had always been at the edge of his life, like when he was a child in Egypt and soldiers slaughtered boys his age in Bethlehem. Now, though, he could see the signs of the predator in faces he saw in the crowd. It was certainly there in the way the high priest's men glared at him while he spoke. Agreements had been made, covenants of some kind. Something taking form against him had become final. He felt the increasing danger. There was a new urgency but he could not seem to get his men to understand.

He responded to the threat as most men would. He sometimes stayed away from Jerusalem. He asked the people he helped not to advertise what he had done for them. He kept to the countryside and to Galilee. He knew the citified priests were less likely to look for him up in the hills, and besides, they probably thought all the Galilean bumpkins would rally in his defense.

If only those Jerusalem priests knew! They were fools, believing old wives' tales about how rustics band together and how interrelated everyone is. He had not even been able to help the people in his own hometown. They questioned who he said he was and remembered only that he was "the carpenter's son." Maybe they meant Mary's Bastard. Or maybe they remembered him only as the boy who had grown up among them and this kept them from believing in his mission. There certainly was no one coming to his defense.

Not even in his family. They had their doubts too. In Capernaum when the crowds pressed around the house he was in and no one had even a moment to eat, what did his family do? They made a plan to take him by force because they thought he was losing his mind. His own mother? His brothers and his sisters? They should have known! So much for any Galileans coming to his aid!

It can't matter now. There are more important things to consider. Judas has gone missing, offended with Mary and the nard. This time, he might be more than just offended.

Let him go. He can't change very much of what is coming. Jesus already knows the rulers are moving against him. There are many reasons. He's a threat. The people follow him and would even crown him king. Such a thing would move the hand of Rome. It is what the rulers fear.

Besides, he was predicted. He's chosen. He does astonishing wonders. And the people love him for it, at least at the moment. Nothing could be more dangerous in the current state of affairs.

What he has planned for the days ahead will make things even worse. He is going to declare himself. Openly. A confrontation of some kind is sure to follow and it is going to happen just as the Holy City is crammed with pilgrims and the governor has reinforced the guard at the Fortress and the ruling council is eager to prove itself to Rome. Some of the Pharisees have secretly warned him. The authorities want him dead.

It is a good time to remember who he is. He is not the usurper that Herod the Great thought he was. He is not Mary's Bastard as some in his hometown think. He's not some misbehaving rabbi as the priests at the temple believe. He is Yeshua ben Joseph of Nazareth, of the tribe of Judah, of the House of King David, servant of the most high God. He is the one predicted. He is the chosen son.

And his moment has come. It is time for him to ascend beyond Bethany.

Urbs:

THE CITY

Jerusalem
The season of Passover
Nisan of the Hebrew Calendar, 3790

Some men live as rootless wanderers all their lives. They never know what it means to belong to a people and a land. Other men feel they belong to many places. They distribute their time and their affection as some men do among numerous lovers.

A very few men know what it is to love a place as though it were a living being. To feel as one with it. To understand it. To love it as though it is almost the meaning of life. To feel its griefs and its joys. To thrill to its pulse and its rhythms.

This is how Yeshua ben Joseph of Nazareth loves Jerusalem.

It is not simply that his life has been intertwined with her, though he was first brought here to be dedicated just weeks after he was born. He has come many times each year since. He can remember the journeys. They punctuated his life, gave it texture, and measured his ascent to manhood.

No, his love for this city is far more than the sum of the three decades of life he has shared with her. It is a love that lives in him because he believes that God lives in Jerusalem.

It has been troubling to him that he has recently been forced to stay away. His life and the lives of his men required it. The conspiracies of the chief priests became public knowledge and there was also the scheming of a new Herod to keep in mind. How long he has had to be wary of men with that name.

Still, he has decided to come now because it is the season of Passover. One hundred thousand pilgrims will soon flood the Holy City, swelling its streets as the melting snows of Mt. Hermon swell the streambeds of Galilee. The usual precautions are already under way. Workers repair roads and strengthen bridges. Temple guards plan for the oncoming throng. Storekeepers lay in new stock while innkeepers sweep out rooms.

The sight of the pilgrims streaming into the city moves him. The faithful travel to Jerusalem from both nearby villages and exotic cities in the far reaches of the empire. To all who come, the land of Israel speaks. She is tiny in comparison to other nations, one hundred and fifty miles from north to south and seventy-five miles from east to west. It means that the imprint of history is somehow condensed, that a man who knows the ancient stories can hardly take a step without stirring a memory of Israel's past. He knows this history, and understands that to be a pilgrim to the Holy City is to enter a liturgy of the land, as though God summons his people to Jerusalem for a journey of centuries as well as of miles.

It is the destination, of course, that gives each pilgrimage its meaning. The Holy City is a sight men and women remember all their lives. She sears the soul with her radiance. To the faithful she is the dwelling place of God; there is no place as magnificent.

He has heard the people of Israel speak of the city the way King Solomon spoke of a woman in *Shir Ha-Shirim*, his song of love. Hours are spent just describing her walls. It is understandable. Jerusalem's walls are seven times the height of a man and are punctuated with magnificently carved gates. Within those gates is little more than a single square mile, home to some twenty-five thousand people. Yet in that space stand buildings that make Jerusalem a breathless sight, a legend of grandeur throughout the empire.

Much of this is the legacy of Herod the Great, though most Jews spit at the mere mention of his name. He was a cruel, ambitious man who heartlessly subdued the people of Jerusalem to appease his masters in Rome. Still, he left a stunning legacy in stone. He built an opulent palace for himself, of course, but he also commissioned the daunting Fortress of Antonia—a tribute to his friend and mentor Mark Antony—and gave it every feature a Roman garrison might need. It is so grand that a highway passes through it and as many as 600 legionnaires can rest comfortably within its walls.

Yet none of these structures begins to compare with the temple, a gleaming vision of grandeur with its gigantic stones, inlaid gold, vast porticos, alabaster spires, and soaring Corinthian columns. It is so huge it occupies almost all of the upper east side of Jerusalem, 12 percent of the entire city. A thousand wagons were needed just to transport her stones. Ten thousand men work on her now.

There are other splendid buildings of course. Jesus has come to love them all in one way or another. The city boasts hundreds of synagogues. There is also the Hasmonean Palace where Herod Antipas—Herod the Great's son—makes his home. It is one of the reasons that Jerusalem is often called "a city of palaces." Always there are the amphitheaters, the markets, and the ornate baths.

Jesus is not deceived, though. He knows what lies behind these magnificent structures. The corruption within them reminds him of the graves that the officials paint white so that no one accidentally touches them and becomes unclean. These graves are pleasant in their brilliance on the outside. Inside they are filled with dead men's bones.

This is how he sees many of the men who lead Israel as if there is no God. They are among the seventy-one men of the Sanhedrin, the seven thousand temple priests, the hundreds of temple guards, the seemingly countless rabbis and the huge variety of civil authorities. What may be eaten, what may be sold, how far a man may walk and on what days, who a man may marry and how he may bury her when she dies, how a man ought to pray, and what his children may inherit are all decided by this Sanhedrin and its army of ever-squabbling experts.

Beneath this heavy hand are the people. As magnificent as Jerusalem is to look upon, it is the people—indeed, all the people of Israel—who have captured his affection. His heart breaks for them. He watches them scurry about the city. He thinks of them sleeping with their children in beds built over the ovens in their homes, their few animals, too valuable to leave to thieves and the cold, sleeping nearby. He thinks of how despised they are. The Roman Empire boasts thirty-one million people, some say as many as fifty million. The Jews account for only 6 to 12 percent of this, four to eight million at most. They are a tiny, odd-seeming, sometimes backward minority to the roiling pagan world and they are seldom allowed to forget it.

So they cling to the faith they have received. They pray. They tithe. They obey the laws of God. If they can, they travel to Jerusalem each year for the feasts. They listen to what the rabbis teach. They fear Rome, suspect their rulers, hope for the coming of the Messiah, and wonder if God still dwells among them or if *ichabod*—"the glory has departed"—will be their epitaph as it was for some of their ancestors.

Jesus watches them now as they make their way to Jerusalem to celebrate the Passover in what the Hebrew calendar tells them is the three thousand, seven hundred, and ninetieth year since the dawn of creation. Most have been coming to the Holy City for the feast as long as they can remember. It has always been as it is now. The hectic roads. The streets of the city thick with crowds. The sleeping bodies filling nearly every empty space.

These, though, are mere inconveniences. More important is the sense of mystery, of the holy, that pervades the city. Each pilgrim is eager to eat of the sacrificial lamb, eager to recall the great deliverance of Israel from captivity. All hope that God sees—and that he cares.

He does. Jesus is certain of it. It is why he has come, but he knows that it is no ordinary Passover that is about to begin in the city. Because Israel's God does see and because he does care, there is soon to be a confrontation. It will seem a severe mercy, but it comes because God has chosen Jerusalem and will not leave her to another—not even to herself.

Imperium:
THE EMPIRE

The road from Caesarea to Jerusalem
The 29th of March, 784 AUC

He is the kind of man who is ever surprised by sincere religion. He's more comfortable with Roman ways. They make sense to him. A citizen offers money to a god for the perfectly understandable reason that he wants good fortune. The man builds a house or plants a field or takes a lengthy journey. He wants it all to go well. He also doesn't want to anger the priests who whisper into the ears of the powerful. They depend on offerings. Demand them, really. So why not reverently place a bag of coins on the altar of Diana, or perhaps Saturn or young Mercury? The more people who see it, the better. Maybe later, a grateful toss to old Bacchus will serve well, too. It is only reasonable—and civilized.

He finds that these Jews aren't as reasonable as this, though.

They are mystifying, and this is why Pontius Pilate, the Prefect of Judea, made such mistakes in the beginning.

He wanted to impress and he wanted to do it immediately upon assuming authority, so when he moved his troops from Caesarea to Jerusalem for the winter he allowed them to carry flagpoles and standards topped with carvings of Tiberius. He thought the old emperor might hear of it and be pleased. He knew the Jews wouldn't be. That's why he did it at night.

It was an act of foolish bluster by a newly minted official. The Jews erupted. Their law forbids "images"—particularly images of a pagan emperor and particularly in their Holy City. The next day multitudes of Jews rushed to Caesarea. They pleaded with the governor to remove the images. Pilate refused, believing it would be an insult to Caesar. The people, too, would not be moved and remained in place, protesting, for six days. Finally, exasperated, Pilate ordered his troops to wade in among the bodies, swords drawn. That's when these Jews stunned him. Even under threat of death, they would not yield. Instead, they bared their necks. *Kill us if you will*, they were saying, *we will not let you defile the city of God*. He had never seen men so aflame with religion, never known a people willing to die merely for a god. It confused him and made him hesitate. Finally, shaken, he ordered the troops and their standards out of Jerusalem and back to Caesarea.

The Jews deemed it a great victory. Rome saw it as a defeat. There could not be another.

Pilate chastised himself for being weak and swore it would not happen again. When the sensitive children of Abraham worked themselves into a frenzy once more—after he announced plans for an aqueduct to be paid for out of temple funds—he had no intention of backing down.

Tens of thousands of Jews gathered to protest and they abused Pilate by name. This was going too far. Pilate disguised his soldiers in civilian clothes and told them to spread out into the crowd. They had clubs and were told to wait for a signal and then to beat the leading protesters in order to drive the mob away. He had specifically said not to use swords, but his men were fed up with these contentious eccentrics and tucked swords into their belts despite his orders. When the signal came, they vented their rage, slashing and cutting until dozens of Jews lay dead.

So began the tense standoff between the Jews of Judea and their new governor.

As peculiar as the Jews are to him, he is a mystery to them as well. He seems to have no public history. Some say he's a Spaniard. Some say he's from Gaul. The rumor in Jerusalem is that he has an ancestor who was a slave. The name "Pilate" is close to *pileus*, the word that denotes the cap worn by freed slaves. He might have been a minor official somewhere or perhaps a merchant who prospered enough to buy his position. No one knows. Perhaps it is all as simple as his marriage. His wife is Claudia Procula and she is rumored to be the granddaughter of Caesar Augustus. It would be all the credentials Pilate would ever need.

Whatever brought him to Judea, he is an odd choice. The last Prefect, Valerius Gratas, failed miserably, largely because he could not control Jerusalem's high priests. This is difficult to understand because Valerius Gratas was responsible for appointing these high priests. Yet each one, having promised cooperation, rebelled. The very last appointment Valerius Gratas made was a man named *Qayapha*—Caiaphas. Of course, everyone knows that appointing Caiaphas is nearly the same as appointing Annas, Caiaphas' father-in-law. Annas rules Caiaphas, just as he has many other matters in Jerusalem since he himself was high priest years ago.

Why send Pilate to replace Valerius Gratas? He is no diplomat. He is practically an atheist. He does not have the tiniest bit of sympathy for the Jews. He vastly prefers Caesarea, the Roman town on the coast of the Great Sea, to the contentious, peculiar ways of Jerusalem. What makes Rome think that Pilate will keep peace better than Valerius Gratas?

No one knows. Typically, Rome feels no obligation to explain itself. There is only its single demand—complete submission to its fierce, crushing rule—and Pontius Pilate has been sent to issue this demand in Judea.

This is why, now, he is leading a great mass of armed men out of Caesarea Maritima and southeastward along the road through Antipatris. For many years, tradition has dictated that the Prefect enter Jerusalem at the head of his troops on the first day of the great festival. It is a majestic display of the empire's military might. Publicly, Rome claims this march is meant to honor the Jewish feast. In truth, it is done to increase the troops at the Fortress Antonia and in a manner that issues a warning: "No insurrections or riots this week. We are here in force."

The Romans are more suspicious of Jerusalem's Jews during this festival than at any other time. Since they see the world largely in political and military terms, the Romans understand the Jewish Passover as a conquered people's celebration of deliverance, as a reenactment of the time the Jewish god set himself against the institution of empire. It makes Pilate and his troops understandably nervous.

Could there be a more perfect time for the Jews to rebel? The great march from Caesarea each year is Rome's preemptive strike against this possibility. It declares in unmistakable terms, "Not this year."

Pilate's regal procession winds its way sixty miles southeastward from the coast to the gates of Jerusalem. His troops—knowing they march behind the man who is Rome itself in this land—work to make an impression. It is not difficult. They are rugged, muscular men in leather and steel. They keep cadence in loud, crunching steps. Magnificent horses prance under the Prefect and his generals, who themselves are adorned in flowing capes and gleaming armor, polished leather and dyed horsehair plumes. Some are trimmed in finely set jewels and gold.

It is no minor squad on some routine errand that marches into Jerusalem this day. The Fortress Antonia usually houses 500 soldiers. Yet Rome remembers when 8,500 men were killed once in a single temple uprising. Caesar's men do not intend to be caught shorthanded. This parade of might is meant to warn, but it is also meant to reinforce an outpost that will be soon be surrounded by as many as two hundred thousand resentful Jews. It is the reason that Pilate now leads hundreds of troops through Jerusalem's gates.

There is also a religious purpose to this unnerving demonstration. As Pilate rides regally into Jerusalem, he represents the emperor. And the emperor is a god. In fact, he is "the Son of God," according to the religion of the empire. He is praised as "lord," "savior," and the author of "peace on earth." At the emperor's death he will ascend to the realm of the gods where he will join them in ruling over men. This is the religion of the state, and Pilate declares it by his presence, by the might under his command and by his utter disdain for all other religions, the religion of the Jews in particular.

He is a conqueror, then, entering a conquered city. The people watch their enemy march freely through their gates, drums pounding and trumpets blaring, and they know they can do nothing. They belong to Rome. Soldiers shove onlookers roughly aside, commanders astride magnificent mounts stare threats at the sullen crowd. Pilate is, as ever, cold and unmoved. He rides past his subjects, eyes fixed. Once inside the gate, he turns south with his bodyguard trailing and reins his horse to a halt before the Praetorium—Herod's Palace, Pilate's headquarters in Jerusalem. His troops march on to the Fortress.

Rome has now arrived.

The deed is done. The message sent. There will be no uprising, there will be no blasphemous rebellion. A greater god rules.

Hail, Tiberius Caesar, the true Son of the true God. He is Lord, and over the contemptible god of Jerusalem in particular.

Despite their nervousness at Rome's strengthened presence, the Jews are relieved that the Prefect has arrived. Now the great feast can begin. If Pilate had stayed in Caesarea, the great feast could not have taken place. The high priest would have been unable to officiate: not without his vestments. They would have remained where they are now—locked in a chest deep in the Fortress Antonia. They are kept there throughout the year. Only during the three main Jewish feasts and only if the Prefect chooses, is this chest unlocked and the high priest allowed to use his vestments. He may keep them no more than eight days. Then they must be returned. They are locked away again, a sign of absolute Roman rule over all things, even religion.

It is degrading, as it is intended to be, and it transforms the annual Roman march into a cruelly scripted exercise in religious humiliation.

Regnum:

THE KINGDOM

The road from Bethany to Jerusalem
The 9th of Nisan, 3790

On the same day as the Roman procession and at nearly the same time that Pontius Pilate, Prefect of Judea, enters Jerusalem from the west, there is another grand procession taking place from the east. It too is scripted. It too is a demonstration of strength. It too signals the victory of a God.

Since the chief priests, Sadducees, Pharisees, and scribes have failed to kill this Jesus—the one the people would make king, the one who embarrasses Israel before Rome—he is making his move upon the Holy City.

He is joined by those who traveled with him from Galilee, as well as those who began following him once he arrived in Bethany. He will use the old caravan road that leads to Jerusalem from Jericho. He will climb the east side of the Mount of Olives and enter the city after descending and crossing the Valley of Kidron on the other side. This is his plan. He has made other plans, as well.

He begins. It is the first day of the feast, a good day to be approaching the city. Before he has gone far, a crowd begins to form. People have recognized him. Some know him from his teaching, others have heard of the Lazarus affair and the miracles he did with wine, fish, and bread. His appearance delights them. They begin to cheer him. He is walking a road often taken by celebrating pilgrims en route to Jerusalem and so the scene does not appear at all odd. The crowd grows and the cheering changes into singing. Soon the throng is large enough to line both sides of his path.

He is still ascending the east side of the mountain when he pauses to speak to two of his men. He tells them to go on to the next village, which is a short distance away. There, they will find a colt that has never been ridden. They are to bring it to him. They obey immediately. It takes only minutes. The two men find a colt tied by a doorway and when someone standing nearby asks what they are doing, they say simply, "The Lord needs it."

The colt is intended as a sign. Its use is not an accident or a last-minute revelation. It is part of a very specific statement, a type of declaration of war. He intends to ride the colt over the crest of the Mount of Olives, down its western slope, through the Valley of Kidron, and into the Holy City. For Jews who witness this or hear of it later, the image of King Solomon riding just such an animal to his coronation will certainly come to mind. The image will also suggest the words of Zechariah:

> Rejoice greatly, Daughter Zion!
> Shout, Daughter Jerusalem!
> See, your king comes to you,
> righteous and victorious,
> lowly and riding on a donkey.

It is a dangerous declaration. *A king has come. He is even now among us. Victorious. Righteous. He is entering Jerusalem.* And yet Pontius Pilate, emissary of the Roman god on earth, is entering Jerusalem from the opposite direction just now, entirely confident of an entirely different dominion. The two processions entering Jerusalem this day promise a clash of deities, a contest of gods and the empires built in their names.

When his men return with the colt, the rabbi climbs upon it and rides over the crest of the mountain. The Holy City is now gloriously in view. Pilgrims on the road coming from Jericho meet other pilgrims coming from Jerusalem in the opposite direction.

They have all heard that the rabbi is in Bethany and they want to see the miracle worker as well as the man he raised from the dead. The crowds merge, blend, part to either side of the path and continue shouting their joy.

In a time-honored act of welcome to royalty, the people lay their robes upon the ground. This forms the carpet due a king. Overhead, the people wave branches they have just torn from trees. They are "preparing the way," demonstrating to this man that they receive him as their ruler.

The passion heightens. The excitement spreads. Soon, the great throng begins chanting the traditional *Hallel* of the Passover liturgy:

> Hosanna!
> Blessed is he who comes in the name of the Lord!
> Blessed is the coming kingdom of our father David!
> Hosanna in the highest heaven!

As the colt descends the eastern side of the mountain, the great mass of pilgrims multiplies. Hundreds of people pour out of the white tents that dot the mountainside, their temporary dwellings during the feast. They eagerly join the celebration, which seems to them no more than a particularly thrilling Passover procession. It continues, the Holy City looming, the crowds thickening.

•━┤━━━

The priests and Pharisees, the scribes and Sadducees, have been watching. They always are. They have been looking for a chance to move on the troublemaker but they choose not to do it during the Feast so as not to arouse the people. This demonstration rankles them though, and they cannot remain quiet and out of view. "Rabbi, rebuke your disciples," they command. They are offended by this praise for a mere man. They know that the words of the *Hallel* pertain to the Messiah.

The young rabbi has already seen these men, already knows their displeasure and their purpose. *I tell you*, he shouts back over the noise and commotion, *if they keep quiet the stones will cry out.*

There. He has said it. If they had been listening they would already have heard him say it many times before. He believes he is the Messiah. He is doing everything possible to declare it, now, on this first day of the feast.

There is nothing more to say. The fool has condemned himself with his own words and in the presence of witnesses. The high priest is right: it is time for this man to die.

The laughter and shouting grows more eager, the waving of branches more frenzied. The rabbi graciously acknowledges it all.

Where the road turns just before an outcropping of rock, the rabbi looks to the city. He grows quiet and reins his colt to a halt. He passes his eyes over Jerusalem as though seeing her for the first time. She is the city of palaces, of his people's kings and their God—now vulnerable in the clenched fist of Rome. He begins to weep. It is not gentle weeping but the loud lament of one in grief. The people hear and grow still. It is a terrible sound and the great throng that was celebrating a moment ago is suddenly paralyzed. Soon, the rabbi speaks. His tone is that of a wounded lover. *How many times I longed to take you in my arms. How very much I have loved you. But you would not receive me. You do not see. You cannot understand. You have grown dull. Soon, armies will encircle you. Your city will be destroyed, your children smashed against the very stones in which you trust. God is coming. The time is now and you are soon to be ruined.*

It is not what the people expect. There is silence, bewilderment, but it does not last. After a pause, the rabbi urges his colt forward and the commotion begins again, moving down the rocky hillside, across the makeshift bridges that span the rushing waters in the Kidron gorge and into the gates of the city. Once inside, the Galilean dismounts. The people press in around him. Some weep. Some dance. More than a few are confused and do not know what to do.

Jesus looks upon them with compassion and sadness. He knows what is coming. Those before him, like heedless sheep herded to slaughter, do not. He can say no more. He turns and begins the short walk to the temple.

He has, then, announced himself.

In a carefully crafted demonstration, the rabbi has declared that he is the true king of Israel. He has scorned the priests, received the worship due only to the Messiah, and prophesied the annihilation of the city. His message is unmistakable: Israel's Prophet-King has come to his people.

He knows also what is taking place on the other side of the city. Rome has come in the form of Pilate and his troops. It occupies in the name of its god. It defies all other deities.

But this is precisely why the rabbi has executed a counter-demonstration. In centuries-old religious symbolism, he has answered the challenge of Rome. *The petty gods of Rome will fall to the God who is Lord of Heaven and Earth. A greater king is now among us. A greater kingdom reigns.*

And that kingdom's self-declared ruler is making his way to the temple of Jerusalem.

Pontifex:
THE PRIEST

House of Caiaphas
The Upper City of Jerusalem
The week of Passover, 3790

The dissident rabbi must die.

This is the conclusion of the old priest who sits in his son-in-law's house on the southwest side of the Holy City. From the compound's well-chosen perch, the grizzled patriarch can look out across the Hinnom Valley to the Bethlehem road. If he turns slightly north, he can pass his weakening eyes over the grandeur of Herod's Palace. A further turn permits him a glimpse of the temple. These scenes have long been the geography of his thoughts, and they are now too as he ponders the difficult thing that must be done.

His name is Annas. He is a small man, as precise in his movements as in his thoughts, as delicate of body as he is ferocious of purpose. He has reasoned his way out of more complex problems than this one but seldom has the danger been as great.

Still, he has seen much and is not easily shaken. The Syrian governor Quirinius appointed him high priest of Jerusalem decades ago. He prospered and grew powerful. His real name, *Hananiah*, means "the Lord has been gracious." As Annas understands it, the Lord has indeed extended his favor.

This comes most noticeably as a gift of perception. He has always understood what others have not. He has always had a way of seeing. What he perceives best is the single great truth that defines his life: the temple in Jerusalem is the key to all power.

This seems perfectly obvious to him. He marvels that so many fools fail to comprehend it. The temple is everything—the biggest enterprise, the holiest ground, and the most revered site in the nation. How can a man know this truth and not make it his servant?

The money alone that passes through the temple is nearly beyond belief. Every single day, great wagonloads of coin—tithes, temple taxes, and the tributes owed to Rome—flow into the temple. She sits at the mouth of a never-ending river of wealth.

For Annas, this means profit. He perceives the potential, and not just from the coins. There is also the trade. He understands what it means that hundreds of thousands of pilgrims make their way to the temple each year—each with gifts, each with needs. There are sacrifices to buy and coins to exchange into the official temple currency. If a person wishes to make a sacrifice, this is what is required. Always, though, there is a fee. Always, there is a percentage for Annas and his family to claim. Even the sacrificial system offers opportunities. Cattle, sheep, olive oil, fruit, birds, grain, wood, cloth for vestments and curtains, gold for utensils— all must be bought, sold, transported, stored, packaged, and made holy by the rituals of priests. All of it costs money, and it can mean riches for the discerning—like Annas.

He began to realize this years ago when the Romans appointed him high priest. It did not take him long to see the beauty in the system. In fewer than ten years, Annas assumed control of the temple markets, made sure every transaction put money into his hands, and bought influence enough to make even the Romans nervous. The Romans, in turn, deposed him, unwilling to feel nervous for long. It did not stop the old schemer. He manipulated, bribed, and cajoled to make sure his sons inherited his position and then he continued to run the temple like a personal kingdom. Now his son-in-law is high priest. Annas controls him so thoroughly that on the streets of Jerusalem people speak of "the high priesthood of Annas and Caiaphas." Everyone knows it is Annas who rules.

Still, he has never confronted anything quite like this current problem. A rabbi from the hills has come down from Galilee and caused trouble in Jerusalem. He has been making wild claims and persuading superstitious people to follow him. His popularity has become a threat—the people might rebel in this rabbi's name and it would force the crushing hand of Rome. Annas is always keenly attentive when a threat to his power looms.

First, the young fool announced himself by riding into the Holy City astride a donkey. He paid people to stand along the roads and shout, "Hosanna! Blessed is the coming kingdom of our ancestor David." The silly pretender was trying to declare himself king by doing what King Solomon had done a millennium ago. He even enlisted a deranged woman to anoint him at a public dinner the evening before.

There were rumors that this holy man could heal. It was all a pretense, of course, but the people, ever eager for some new trick, believed in the rube and his magic. He pretended to heal even on the Sabbath and urged others to ignore the laws of *Shabbat* as well. He justified all of this by twisting Isaiah's song of the vineyard, using it to show that Israel's religious leaders were corrupt.

Men should turn to a new law, the radical insisted. This sent the Pharisees over the edge.

Annas is a Sadducee, though—cool and broad-minded and doubting—so he isn't quickly stirred. Even when rumors arose that the backwoods rabbi raised a dead man in Bethany, Annas remained precise in his plans, measured in his words. He would not have the public—or his enemies—see him nervous.

His patience paid off. The foolish Galilean couldn't help himself. He overplayed his hand. He made the move that confirmed to Annas what he was really up to. What the man truly had in mind, his accusations and his fake miracles aside, was a cut of the temple trade.

That upheaval in the temple is what revealed the truth. It happened suddenly and on the kind of crowded, loud, chaotic day that always precedes Passover. The temple courts were filled with pilgrims and *shulchanim*, moneychangers, just the way Annas likes them to be. The rows of Corinthian columns in the Court of the Gentiles had proven a perfect arcade for the *Chanoyoth*, the exchange booths. Pilgrims could convert their home currency into the official coin of the temple with ease. Annas delighted to see it. He was profiting from every transaction. None of the *shulchanim* conducted business without the old man's permission and without paying the old man's fee. In addition, there was the percentage he demanded from each exchange. It was a profitable arrangement.

Annas also controlled each *mumcheh*, the "one approved" to assure the Levitical fitness of animals for sacrifice. This too was profitable. The *mumcheh* charged a fee for his services, of course, and most were not beyond taking a little extra on the side to approve a damaged beast. It meant the owner could sell his finer animals in the market for profit and offer the ritually unclean ones to God. What was the harm?

These dealings make the temple courts a great riot of trade, all orchestrated by the father-in-law of the sitting high priest. Men weigh coins, argue their value, make calculations, and grandly gesture in market dramas familiar through the centuries. It has been going on for so long that no one remembers when moneychangers did not sit in stalls behind great stacks of coins, when the protests of oxen did not challenge the sound of bickering men. Doves by the thousands coo and sheep bleat and the sound of men squishing their way through manure completes the profitable commotion. It is all music to Annas' ears.

The old man is in such control of these stalls in the Court of the Gentiles that the people secretly call them "The Bazaars of the Family of Annas." They mirror the family greed. Prices are inflated, the poor are targeted, the simple are manipulated, and always there is the extra percentage, the fee off the books, the kickbacks to the conspiring and powerful. Syndicates form. Enforcers arise. Arrangements are understood. It is the Empire of Annas.

That rabbi from the hills knows all this. When he stepped into the temple court that day and started his demonstration, he wasn't trying to bring reform. He was making a move for territory, an obvious grab for power. Feigning outrage, the intruder fashioned a whip from reeds he found on the marble floor and rushed at the moneychangers. He swung wildly with knotted reeds in one hand while he grabbed for change boxes and stacks of coins with the other. He flipped tables into the air with the strength of a carpenter's arm. Benches went airborne. Account books flew at bystanders. Terror filled the courtyard.

It was a criminal disruption of trade. The Mad Rabbi would not let honest workers carry goods through the courts. He sent merchants screaming and pilgrims rushing for safety. It was sacrilege. Sheep spilled out of their pens and doves flew low and loud into the faces of panicked men. Moneychangers racing for safety fell clumsily over their fellow merchants who were crawling the floor to gather spilled coins. The man kept screaming about his "father" and a "den of thieves" and how the Gentiles were supposed to have a House of Prayer in the Temple of God.

It was all a show. Annas knows what the man was really doing: moving into the high priest's terrain. And it has to stop. Forever. He cannot let this man cut into his trade, cannot allow the people to be deceived. How would it look if he lost control to one of the *pagani*, the word the Romans use for people from the country.

He has decided the matter. He has already formed a coalition. The Sanhedrin is no problem, for they will certainly follow his lead. They always do. Together they can maneuver that blasphemer Pilate to use the *ius gladii*—the "supreme jurisdiction" the emperor gives him over the sentence of death—to permanently silence this criminal. Finally, the righteous will be rid of distraction and Annas' market will thrive as before.

The old man pondering the world from his son-in-law's house is at peace. Yet again he feels the power of the gift. He has seen what others have not and has crafted a strategy, a plan sure to safeguard his family's control. No one else is up to the task. It falls to him.

The hills and steep valleys beyond his son-in-law's house speak to him now as they always have. They stand quiet testimony to the unshakeable truth of history: only what remains is of value. Annas intends that his family shall remain—always.

And so it is decided—because Annas has decided it. *What is best for Israel is that this dissident rabbi should die.*

Advenae:

THE FOREIGNERS

Bethany, the Mount of Olives,
and the Court of the Gentiles
at the Temple in Jerusalem
10th of Nisan, 3790

The Gentiles are the issue.

The rabbi has often tried to explain this to his men.

It's about the treatment of the Gentiles.

The Pharisees, the Sadducees, the scribes, and even the Essenes—none of them understand this. They think the rabbi's eruption in the temple was about money and control. It wasn't. It was about the Gentiles, Israel's racism, and the glory of God on earth.

Jesus became enraged when he saw what was happening. It was heartbreaking. There were Gentiles from all over the world at the temple. Some were Greeks who had traveled many days by ship. Some had come with caravans—Elamites, Persians, and Medes among them. Still others, like the Scythians, had thundered across the northern grasslands. They had all risked great distances to worship their God in Jerusalem.

Yet when they arrived at the temple, there was no place for them. There were sheep where the faithful from Crete should have been and tables of the *shulchanim*, the moneychangers, where Ethiopians had a right to pray. Instead of being welcomed to a court prepared for them in the house of God, these Gentiles were nearly in the streets.

It grieved him.

Some temple priests seem to have forgotten—or perhaps agreed to ignore—the very purpose of the temple courts. They are meant to protect the holy from the unclean, it is true, but they are also meant to offer a place to all God-fearing people. It is the reason the temple was made with a series of courtyards. They define how far a worshipper may go toward the Most Holy Place, and where they may stand when they meet with God.

It is an ingenious architectural system, based upon the commandments of the law. Every man has his appointed place. Only the high priest dressed in his vestments may enter the Holy of Holies, of course. Outside is a court reserved for priests. The court beyond is only for Jewish men. Next to it is the Court of the Women. The outermost court, though, is called the Court of the

Gentiles. It bears that name because it is the only courtyard open to Gentiles. It is as close as they can get to the Holy of Holies.

The name is a lie, though. There is no court reserved for the Gentiles now. Indeed, from the moment a foreigner nears the temple today he is threatened and held in suspicion. It starts with the sign at the entrance to the temple grounds, which reads:

> Foreigners must not enter inside the balustrade
> or into the forecourt around the sanctuary.
> Whoever is caught will have himself to blame
> for his ensuing death.

This chilly reception continues inside. Since most Jews must ritually purify themselves before entering the temple, they are careful not to risk contamination. They cannot touch a Gentile or they will become ritually unclean. Nor can they touch what a Gentile has touched. Most Jews won't even speak to a Gentile near the temple. It is only the Temple Guard that pays any attention and then only to make sure the Gentiles don't misbehave.

It would all be worth braving, though, if a foreigner could finally end up in the court of God, free to worship and pray.

Instead, what he finds is a market as unruly as any in Rome.

Rather than cool marbled spaces bordered by soaring Corinthian columns, he finds arguing merchants, complaining animals, and makeshift booths. Rather than shaded alcoves and broad, peaceful walkways, he finds jabbering men carrying goods, the clinking of coins, and the stench of manure. It is nothing like the peaceful, holy place God intends. As important, it does not symbolize the care of Israel's God for those outside of Israel.

This is what stirred Jesus. He was not in an unholy rage. He had not lost control. He was not trying to seize territory. He was certainly not trying to encourage a riot. He was particularly careful not to condemn money changing or the selling of animals for sacrifice. Of all people, he knows these practices are commanded. The law allows Jews to come from distant places to the temple and to bring their local currency. Once they arrive, they can exchange their native currency for the official temple coin, the Tyrian silver shekel. It is troubling enough that the people of Israel have to use this particular coin. It reminds them of how much Tyre hates all Jews. Jesus would never add to his people's burden by condemning what God allows. Nor would he distort the law.

No, what angered him—as it does now—is where the high priest has callously placed the market. He has moved it from the streets to the Court of the Gentiles, the one holy spot on earth reserved for non-Jews. The skimming and the graft, all orchestrated by the high priest's family—yes, the rabbi knows of this—have made a corrupt marketplace of God's house.

This is exactly what Yeshua said while he tried to drive the hard-hearted merchants away. Some of the pilgrims watching him probably did not understand. The priests did, though, and so did the scribes. They recognized his meaning well beyond his exact words.

As he whipped and overturned, he kept shouting, "'My house will be a house of prayer;' but you have made it 'a den of robbers.'" He was blending two sayings from the prophets. He accused the corrupt merchants with a phrase they would know from the prophet Jeremiah. They had indeed made God's house into a "den of robbers," a hideout of thieves.

What stung the most was the rabbi's reference to Isaiah's "house of prayer" image. Many who heard him in the courtyard that day probably thought he wanted the merchants to stop their selling and pray. The educated ones knew better. In rabbinic teaching, when a verse of scripture is quoted, the entire context of the saying is meant to be applied. Rabbi Yeshua did not mean to cite just three words from Isaiah's lips. He meant to invoke the entire passage that encases those three words. Every Israelite in the temple court should have felt the shame.

Let no foreigner who is bound to the LORD say,

"The LORD will surely exclude me from his people."

And let no eunuch complain,

"I am only a dry tree."

For this is what the LORD says:

"To the eunuchs who keep my Sabbaths . . .

to them I will give within my temple and its walls

a memorial and a name

better than sons and daughters . . .

And foreigners who bind themselves to the LORD

to minister to him,

to love the name of the LORD,

and to be his servants . . .

these I will bring to my holy mountain

and give them joy in my house of prayer . . .

for my house will be called

a house of prayer for all nations.

His meaning could not have been clearer, especially to the priests. There is theft and bribery taking place in the temple courts. It makes the whole house of God into a hideout for thieves. Even worse, the location of this dishonest trade drives the Gentiles away. This is despite God's promise that the Gentiles will always have a place.

Now, a crass market occupies that place. This means more than just that foreigners must find a new place to pray. It means that God's intentions for the nations of the earth are not represented in his temple. It means that Gentiles will look to the Holy City but see no sign they will ever be counted there among God's people.

There could hardly be a more important issue. The fate of the nations is in this seemingly small matter of where a Jerusalem market operates. It is no wonder Jesus roared at the merchants. The nations are at stake.

He was doing something else as he pushed moneychangers and sheep from the temple courts and it, too, was risky. He was challenging a syndicate. He was putting a powerful criminal enterprise on notice. He knows what this might mean, what the chief priests and their merchant friends are saying even now.

This outsider wants us to clear the Gentile court of all trade. He's willing to say so publicly, to make trouble unless we do. Surely he knows it will never happen. The merchants would riot. Rome would be enraged, since it also profits from the markets. And Annas would have our heads, particularly because he has already told us what we should do. For the sake of the temple and the nation, this loudmouthed rabbi should be killed.

From the beginning, it was about the Gentiles. And now, much of what is about to occur is for the Gentiles too.

IX

Coniuratus:

THE CONSPIRACY

If time could stand still, if it were possible to stop a moment in the life of Jesus as though freezing it in the ice of a Mt. Hermon winter, there is one moment that would be among the most revealing. It is the very last second of his attempt to claim the outer court of the temple for the Gentiles.

If this were possible, merchants searching for coins, pilgrims running in fear, doves flying erratically in panic, sheep attempting to leap one another to safety, tables turning in midair, coins bouncing in every direction, priests running for help, temple guards running toward Yeshua, his men wary of the danger, booths toppling over—would instantly stop in mid-motion. All would be suddenly quiet and still.

The revelation would be in the faces of the chief priests. They would be standing at a distance, only slightly affected by the commotion. The look on their faces would be one of disgust blended with knowing and a sense of satisfaction.

It would be because they have information others in that courtyard do not. It is this: Jesus is a dead man. This deed, this outrage in the temple, has sealed his fate. He was already a target, though before now there were still options, variations in how his future might play out. Now his fate has been decided. Instantly. With no turning back. The leading men already know this man will be killed and killed horribly in a matter of days.

Jesus knows it too.

He has been hunted all his life. He grew up hearing his parents' stories of how a wicked, dying king sent men to murder him when he had barely left his mother's breast. Infant boys in Bethlehem died in his stead. His parents wisely hid him in Egypt. Even when he returned to his country, the son of the wicked king ruled and instilled such fear that the family did not return to Bethlehem. Instead, they moved him a hundred miles away, toward the mountains of the north.

He was not safe even then. This son of Herod, Archelaus, still wanted him dead. The notoriously brutal ruler of Judea had apparently learned from his father or the magician-priests from the east or perhaps the scholars in his own court that a boy born in Bethlehem had been a threat and might still be. Archelaus lived until Jesus was eight. The boy's parents must have thought about the evil possibilities every night of those years.

While authorities hunted him, he was also in danger from people offended by his teaching. He had just begun appearing in public when he decided to speak in his hometown. The locals were proud of him and kept bringing up stories from his youth. He wasn't Mary's Bastard anymore. Then it went badly. He spoke in the synagogue and decided to mention one of his favorite themes: God and the Gentiles. The people rioted. They surrounded him, shouting and threatening, and drove him to the edge of a cliff he knew well from his adventures as a boy. They had every intention of murdering him—these people whose faces filled his memories and who were among his closest friends. Given who he was, he simply walked away but the experience was so disturbing that he recounted it to his men.

Once the officials in Jerusalem became aware of him, they began envisioning his death. If he healed a man on the Sabbath, they plotted. If he called God his father, they talked murder. If he taught something new, they planned assassination. They were hesitant, weak, and ever debating, but they were certain they could not survive if they did not take his life.

He did not cower before them. He stayed away from Jerusalem for a season and based his ministry in the north for a while. This simply made sense. It kept his men from harm and meant less time debating the Pharisees in Jerusalem and more time teaching and healing among the people.

Still, he did not hesitate to face down those who wanted him dead. He once openly asked a crowd why they were planning to kill him. This was in the temple and while the chief priests were watching. He almost casually asked yet another crowd the same thing. No one denied it. Some Pharisees told him that Herod Antipas wanted to kill him and they urged him to move away. Jesus called the old conniver a "fox," and then started talking about his mission and his death.

He seemed fearless. He taught. He did miracles. He preached against the scandalous men in control of the temple. It became an embarrassment to the conspirators. Everyone knew the religious leaders wanted him killed, and yet he appeared openly in the temple and taught ever more radical ideas. They were unable to take him. He was somehow protected, operatives reported to their masters. The people of Jerusalem discussed it openly. Yeshua's enemies simply could not do him harm. Not yet.

Months of this standoff went by. The leaders plotted—incompetently, ever talking—but unable to act. The rabbi went about his business, the possibility of death hanging over him. In fact, he talked about his death constantly. His men were tortured by the thought but he knew it was vital that he predict his murder, explain its meaning, and prepare his followers for what would happen once he was gone.

Whatever plans the officials had made, Jesus decided to force their hand. He rode down the Mount of Olives on a donkey and entered the city at the same time that Pilate was entering at the head of his troops on the other side. It was the first day of the festival. Everyone knew what it meant. He was proclaiming himself king. The pilgrims who camped around the Kidron loved it and cheered him. Then he made his way to the temple. Everyone was eager to see what he would do. But he did nothing. He looked around for a moment and then left. Perhaps he was testing them, pondering his options.

The next day was no test. He entered the temple courts early on that second morning. He didn't hold back. He immediately ran the merchants from the outer court and . . .

The frozen moment has come. What shows in the chief priests' unmoving faces is the certain knowledge that this man's death can no longer wait. Killing him after the feast might prove too late. He is too dangerous. He has directly challenged their authority. He has compromised them in the eyes of the people. He has somehow made himself one with God and the temple. Though he does not mention the Annas syndicate by name, he attacks its methods. More dangerous still, if he led a rebellion and proclaimed himself king, the Romans would decimate the nation.

The frozen moment just at the end of the temple clearing is not frozen, of course. So it races by, no more than a fleeting moment of meaning on a priest's face. Yet after this moment, nothing is the same. The religious leaders, already engaged in a conspiracy, feel themselves under siege. They can wait no longer to execute the rabbi. Matters have become too desperate. The man will have to die. Even if the people have to see. Even if it has to happen during the feast.

Still, it should not be hard. They have already heard from someone willing to betray him. They will need to ask for help from the Romans, of course. Only the Romans have the troops to stave off a riot and only their governor can issue a sentence of death. But the Romans are always more compliant at feast times. *No, it has to be now. Take him at night, sentence him, and end him without further hesitation. That is the plan.*

None of this will come as a surprise to Jesus. He has been predicting it for years. And he's had a long season of preparation. Powerful men have been trying to kill him all of his life.

Now, he intends to let them.

X

Occursus:
THE MEETING

House of Caiaphas
Upper City
Jerusalem
First week of Nisan, 3790

Caiaphas is a wealthy man. He's been fortunate. His father-in-law, Annas, acquired money and power for the family during the nine years he was high priest. Though the Romans saw him as a threat and removed him, his fortune has served Caiaphas well. The family grew more prosperous still and rose in the right circles of power. They are among the aristocratic families of Judea who prosper through their priestly connections. Caiaphas has heard his father-in-law insist upon it often: *The temple is the nation's source of power and the priests control the temple.* The old man would do anything to strengthen his family's control. He has married his children into the best families and made sure money has reached the right hands. There is little he would not do for power.

All of this has served to make Caiaphas a high priest. It is a rich man's role. Even aside from the bribes and the constant campaigning, the high priesthood is a costly position. The man who holds the seat is expected to make lavish sacrifices at the temple each year, particularly on the Day of Atonement. The bills are huge. There is also the cost of servants, the cost of feasting the governor and, of course, the cost of the proper robes and adornments. Together, it amounts to a fortune.

Yet Caiaphas has done well. He has been high priest for fifteen years. It is an accomplishment, particularly since he serves at the pleasure of the fickle, demanding Romans. He has learned how to finesse them, how to soothe the savage soul of the empire. He has even come to terms with Pilate. It helps that Caiaphas never fails to offer a bull and a lamb—every day—for the emperor and the people of Rome. The Romans insist upon it, and Caiaphas fulfills his duty despite the outrage of other priests. He has also kept a tricky but workable tension with the Pharisees, who are ever in a stir about some trifle of the law.

Impressive rewards come to a wise high priest and Caiaphas has worked hard to be wise. He lives in a mansion in the Upper City with numerous servants and enviable grounds. His position allows him to put his relatives in choice positions of power—like temple treasurer. Annas taught him well, so he has learned how to expand his control and increase his percentage of the trade in the lively temple markets. There is no reason his sons, and their sons after them, should not be able to do the same.

They will, however, need to keep an eye on Rome. These people are sensitive about their gods, their Caesars, and receiving all due honor. They don't like the Jews and they don't understand the narrowly religious. They find the Torah to be filled with myths and the laws of God to be offensive, particularly those laws that make Jews treat Romans like something to be scraped off of a sandal. If any of this goes wrong, it can mean blood, even loss of money or power to the ruling families.

●◀▬▬▬➤

This is precisely why Caiaphas has been insistent about the troublemaker Jesus. He has become so concerned he is convening a meeting today at his house. He warned the leaders and then he warned them again: this man is different and has to be dealt with. Annas had warned Caiaphas, and Caiaphas in turn warned the Sanhedrin. They were like children though—squeamish and incompetent. The Pharisees tried to kill the Galilean when he first became public. The bumblers could not do the job. Then the

Herodians joined them. Together they still failed. Ever since, the trickster has been roaming the nation at will.

Now, the matter has become a crisis. Days ago this Jesus concocted a scheme to make it appear that he had brought a man back from the dead. Some fellow helped him—a man from Bethany named Lazarus. The people went crazy with delight. Now the Galilean's support is broadening and it is happening at the worst possible time: at Passover, when pilgrims flood by the thousands into the city. It is a bad time to have a rogue rabbi stirring things up. And it hasn't escaped anyone's notice that this particular rabbi speaks openly against priests, the temple, and even the law.

This crisis called for an emergency meeting. The elders have been summoned, as well as the top scribes and the priests who work for Caiaphas. The leaders of the opposition party, the Pharisees, will also be there.

This is important. There has to be a consensus. The Pharisees are too popular with the masses to be left out but Caiaphas never has understood their appeal. With all their rules and their intricate little systems overlaid on the law, it is a wonder anyone follows them. Perhaps it's their reputation for being a popular front, for being reformers. Most of their leaders come from rural villages, live simply, and seem to care about doing God's will. The people probably admire them because they are everything the usual temple priests are not: zealous, disciplined, and holy—in their own way.

Caiaphas is a Sadducee. His party is more influential among the upper classes. This suits him. To be a Sadducee requires intelligence and a broader understanding of the world that the people just don't have. The elite and sophisticated are Caiaphas' tribe. Besides, they are the Israelites with money.

It is probably best that things remain as they are: the Sadducees tending the aristocrats, and the Pharisees appealing to the people. Both parties are effective at what they do. The Sadducees hone religion to an acceptable minimum. They rework the mystical aspects of religion into something reasonable, something more compatible with life. The Pharisees might win the people with their zeal, their tales of a divine predestination and their certainty about supernatural things. Caiaphas finds it all too fantastical. He lives in the real world. He doesn't believe that the future is determined. He doesn't rely on the rescue of miracles. And he will not be forced to believe that every holy book floating about is to be taken as scripture. He'll remain in the safe confines of the Torah— as the Sadducees have learned to interpret it.

These theological differences are part of the reason he has called the meeting today. The whole city is ablaze with the news of this Lazarus coming back to life. Of course, it is all an illusion concocted by the rebellious rabbi, but for the people to believe in resurrections is a threat to the Sadducees more than anyone else. The Sadducees know such things do not occur, so a widespread resurrectionist movement could erode their base of power.

The appointed number has now assembled in the high priest's home. The formal greetings are offered, the seatings by rank are made. Now the worrying can begin.

What is to be done? This man's popularity is greater than ever and it is because he does such astounding wonders. The people are rallying to him.

There is much nodding and rubbing of chins.

The Romans won't have it. They'll think this radical is leading a rebellion—which he probably intends to do—and they'll convince themselves that all Jews are under his influence. We'll lose our place and the Romans will crush the nation.

Caiaphas has heard this kind of fearful prater for years. The Pharisees may believe in divine preordaining but it certainly hasn't made them courageous.

"You know nothing at all!" he explodes. "You do not understand!" This is typical Sadducee rudeness. They're famous for it.

"It is better for you to have one man die for the people than to have the whole nation destroyed!" Caiaphas is incensed. *These men are idiots. The frustration of it! Why can't they ever see their way to a solution? And act!*

The other leaders do see the danger. The feast is upon them. The Romans will reinforce Antonia. And the city's population will increase five times. It comes just when the masses talk about almost nothing else but the mystical powers of this Jesus.

It is a time for cool heads and, perhaps, cooler hearts.

Here is the conclusion of the matter: Kill him. Kill them both—this Jesus and this man Lazarus. End the threat. Then there will be no more of this pretend Messiah and his sidekick telling the world the dead have come back to life. Kill them. Kill them now.

This last phrase causes the nervous among them to urge caution. *Kill* them, *but do it in secret. You don't want to incite the people, particularly the easily influenced simpletons from the country-side. They would riot and all would be lost.*

All nod agreement. The meeting is done. It occurs to more than a few among them that they have made such plans before. Nothing has come of them.

Caiaphas worries that once again the Galilean will be allowed to slip away. During the two days since the meeting, things have only gotten worse. This Jesus entered the city on the first day of the feast and in such a bold manner that no one missed his meaning: he thinks he's the rightful king. Huge crowds gathered around him as he rode a donkey from the east through the city gates. The idiot somehow thinks he's Solomon! Now, between the rumors he raises the dead and his announcement that he is king, the whole situation is becoming even more dangerous than it was before.

The high priest worries. Then comes news. A messenger at the door brings word from the temple: *One of the rabbi's men will lead us to him. He asks little. It seems he has become disillusioned with the one he has been following. With your permission, we'll finalize plans.*

Caiaphas is pleased. His permission? Of course. Nothing could be better than executing this Jesus and laying the blame on one of his own men. Proceed.

•◄▬▬

The man breaking away from the Galilean troublemaker is Judas Iscariot—*Ish Kerioth*, a "man of Kerioth." It is a town nearby, in Judea. He is the only one of the rabbi's followers who is not from the north. It might be part of the reason he feels apart from them now. None of the rest seem to have trouble with their leader's behavior.

He was eager to be one of Jesus' men at the beginning, but it was not long before things went badly. *The man just started teaching such odd things.* He insisted that the only way to draw near to God was to eat his flesh and drink his blood. *Who would demand such a thing?* He allowed women to travel with him who tended his needs and gave him huge amounts of money. And as the rabbi grew more popular, the money poured in. Judas would know. He was the treasurer.

It was in the authority of this role that Judas broke with the rabbi. *It was clearly a matter of sin.* Just last night, in Bethany, a woman poured a year's wages worth of perfume on Jesus while he just sat there taking it in. She unbound her hair and knelt at his side. *And that was before she touched him!*—using her hair to rub nard on his feet. *It was an outrage.*

It shouldn't go without mention that the woman was the sister of Lazarus—the man the rabbi claimed to bring back from the dead. Judas expressed his disgust at the moment and then left, certain that everyone in the room thought as he did: the woman's actions were shameful. He alone had the courage to get up and leave.

He thought about it as he went and then he knew exactly what to do. It is the reason he has come to the high priests tonight. "What are you willing to give me if I deliver him over to you?"

The chief priests and the temple guard ask him to wait. They secure approval from Caiaphas and offer a price. Whether Judas knows it or not, this price has great symbolic meaning. It is likely what the priests intend.

Thirty pieces of silver. There could hardly be a more demeaning price. It is the standard rate for the purchase of a slave.

Oraculum :
THE TEACHINGS

Judea, Samaria, Galilee
3787 to 3790

Looking back upon it now, it does not seem there was ever a chance it was going to work. He had not come to get along with them. He had come to change everything. They, in turn, would never give up what they had—and they knew he meant to expose them. There was simply never going to be peace between Jesus and the rulers of Israel.

How nice it might be now had he felt he could be more . . . *gentle*. Did he need to hit them so hard? Was it really important that the changes should come all at once? He could have sat with them as he once did when he was a child. He might have honored the old ones, maybe spent some years at their side. He might have won them over to a less cynical, less compromising way.

But no. He was a reformer. They were entrenched. He was a

purist. They thought in terms of the greater good, the larger picture, the less strident way. He thought them evil. They thought him unclean. He said God opposed them. They knew God never speaks through bastards.

It was this way from the beginning. He had hardly started his public work before he went straight to Jerusalem, stormed into the temple and forced out the merchants. It is exactly what he did just a few days ago at the start of the feast—and it wasn't received well either time.

Shortly after that first temple episode, he decided to leave the city and go home to Galilee. Instead of going around Samaria to get there—like most Jews do, to avoid the heretic half-breed Samaritans—he went straight through Samaria and ended up at a well talking to a woman. His own men were scandalized, so of course the chief priests and rulers in Jerusalem heard. They were already upset by the way he had treated a member of the Sanhedrin. After rebuking the man for ignorance, he told him he had to be "born again." Who was he to speak to a member of the council in this way!

He was obviously trying to put his finger in the very places they were sensitive. He went to Jerusalem and healed a lame man on the Sabbath. He defended it, but it was not hard to understand why the officials thought he could have done it another day: the man had been sitting in that exact spot for thirty-eight years! Then, on another Sabbath, he decided to pick grain. It is forbidden and he knew it, but that was just before he healed a man's hand on yet another Sabbath. None of these cases were emergencies. He was obviously making a point.

He started drawing such large crowds that he had to speak from mountainsides. This was mainly because of the healings. Even Roman officers came to him. People said he'd even brought a widow's son back from the dead.

He couldn't avoid controversy. He didn't want to. A woman with a colorful past poured perfume over him and then used her hair to wipe her tears into his feet. He was having dinner in the home of a Pharisee at the time. It was bound to become a scandal. And it did. He also seemed to be changing. His mother and brothers went to a house where he was teaching and sent word that they wanted to see him outside. He wouldn't go. He said that everyone in the house was his family. Even his followers and defenders couldn't understand this.

It made the officials nervous that he appeared to teach in code. He didn't cite rabbi after rabbi, scholar after scholar, as other teachers did. He told stories about seeds, crops, fish, wine, and people of nearly every profession. He once told a story about dirt. The priests couldn't understand him but they were sure he was planning a rebellion.

That's when they started trying to kill him.

But he ignored them. He kept healing and teaching and bringing back the dead and overpowering demons. His men said he once walked on water and that he fed thousands of people from a tiny bit of food. His radical ideas and the amazing things he did were the talk of the nation.

He was careful, though, and smart. When the teachers tried to maneuver him into saying the righteous shouldn't pay taxes, his answer impressed even the experts. When the people tried to make him king by force, he hid. He knew it wasn't his time and that an insurrection wasn't the right way.

His teaching was the revolution he intended. He told an adulteress her sins were forgiven. The law said she should be killed. He said that a blind man's blindness wasn't caused by sin. This turned their teaching on its head. He said that true righteousness was a matter of inner things. The officials had worked hard to make religion about rituals and obedience—the outer life of a man. They weren't happy he was undoing their work.

He went further. A kingdom from God would soon replace

Rome. A new religious order was dawning. He told his crowds not to follow the scribes and the Pharisees. Then he started challenging the idea of "unclean." He made a Samaritan the hero of one of his stories. He ate with criminals and showed kindness to Gentiles. He called a Syrophoenician woman a dog—but then immediately drove demons from her daughter.

He kept hammering away at these themes right up to the time he set out for Jerusalem. By then he was talking a great deal about his death.

It's obvious now. They were never going to understand him. It was never going to work. The surprise is they haven't killed him already.

It is hard to describe how much they hated him. Even before they conspired to murder him, they bombarded him with insults and lies. They couldn't stop using the word "bastard." They accused him of having a demon and of being a Samaritan. They thought it would upset him. It didn't. He never even bothered to respond. They kept on accusing. He was a sinner, a blasphemer, a drunk, a glutton, a Sabbath breaker, and a false prophet. They were vicious, but not as vicious as they were going to be. He had yet to do the things that would offend them most.

He never spared them, never backed down. He called them blind guides and hypocrites. He said that they were like their father the devil and he compared them to serpents. They loved their traditions more than scripture, he charged, and he urged the people to simply ignore them. He even told the chief priests that the kingdom was going to be taken from them and given to another nation. They assumed he meant the Gentiles. There was nothing they found as offensive.

That was it. They wanted him dead.

Once he arrived in Jerusalem, he was obviously looking for a fight. When he brought his friend Lazarus back from the dead in Bethany, he had to know they were looking for him. It would have been a good time to stay out of view. He couldn't do it. Again, he allowed a woman to pour perfume on him and touch him with her hair. Again, he emptied the Court of the Gentiles, and this after he entered Jerusalem using all the traditional symbols to declare himself king.

It still wasn't enough for him. He didn't go sit quietly somewhere and wait for them to come. No. He went to the temple and kept calling for change—right in front of the powerful men who wanted him dead. It simply could not have gone any other way.

What they didn't see, what they never heard, was how much it would have pleased him if it had gone another way. There was that image he spoke of once. It was tender and almost painful in its longing and regret. He was speaking to the city as though it was a living being. He often did this, and when he did it was easy to see how he loved.

He said in great, sorrowful tones that he had often wanted to gather Jerusalem's children. This alone was comforting, because he had predicted the suffering of the nation's young many times. Then, that wonderful image: "How often I have longed to gather your children together, as a hen gathers her chicks under her wings."

We can imagine him pondering this. It would have been late on an afternoon and the smell of rain would fill the air. An unusually cool breeze would warn of what was coming. There, in a village street or near a barn, little chicks would scurry about in fear, not knowing what to do before the coming rain. A hen, their mother, would raise her wings slightly and urge the chicks underneath. If necessary, she would brush one or two roughly against her body so they wouldn't be lost. The chicks would be warm and protected while the mother hen endured what came.

He had seen this more than once and each time it felt somehow familiar. It was what he wanted for Israel; that they would know where to turn, find the one who was eager to gather them. He described this to remind them that he had not always been harsh, had not only chastised and condemned.

But they had moved so far from God that they no longer knew his ways or could recognize one he had sent to be among them. They had made religion into something unholy, something monstrous. How else should a righteous God deal with them? They covered his truth with traditions of their own. They turned the holy temple into a haven for criminals. The poor and hurting went untended while twice a day their priests made sacrifices for the emperor of Rome.

"I have longed to gather you," he said in that raw, piercing moment. And then: "But you were not willing!"

So it has not happened. Perhaps it wasn't destined to be in just that way. But he longed for it. And now, he has found a way to show them that he longs for it still.

Proditio:

THE BETRAYAL

Jerusalem
14th of Nisan, 3790

The young man stumbles through the cold night air, clinging desperately to the linen sheets he threw around himself before rushing out the door. The soldiers had come looking for Jesus. The commotion awakened him. There wasn't much time. He knew he had to warn the rabbi. Now, he is not sure he is entirely covered and while he clumsily makes his way through the stony streets he pulls at his makeshift clothes.

He must be careful not to expose himself. He watches warily for bands of soldiers as he tries to avoid the thousands of pilgrims who have settled for the night in the public places of Jerusalem. Some are slumbering in makeshift shelters. Some are huddled around fires. Few notice him. He is grateful. He can feel the cold air on his private parts and worries as he hops and weaves that he is doing something inadvertently shameful. In his native language, "shameful" and "naked" mean the same thing. He cannot know it now, but there will soon come much shame in this night.

He knows where he must go and quickly—to the garden beside the olive press at the foot of the eastern mountain. It is one of the rabbi's favorite retreats, an enclosed, quiet spot where he often meets with his men. The owner offered it as a haven from the stir of the city. Jesus is free to use it whenever he wishes. Its high walls, lush fruit trees, and shrubs make it both pleasant and safe. There may also be something about the tortured way the trunks of the olive trees reach heavenward that holds the rabbi's fascination as well.

The boy composes himself so as not to draw the attention of the guards at the city gate. He walks by, trying to appear as though his world is not shattering. Once past the gatekeepers, he resumes his hopping and weaving. He must hurry. Jesus and his men went this way long ago. He must make up the time.

He descends into the black of the Valley of Kidron. The boy focuses his attention on crossing at one of the temporary bridges. He likely does not think about how the priests discard the remains of the temple sacrifices into the Kidron. He almost certainly is not pondering themes of redemption. He is more likely thinking about failure—his own failure to be there, now, at the rabbi's side.

The boy scurries across the stream and some distance up the Mount of Olives. He knows the path well. He has taken it often. He makes his way through the thick underbrush, into the familiar gated garden and to the far side where the teacher and his men usually rest.

He is sweaty and chilled at the same time, breathless yet determined. He looks for the rabbi amidst the trees and the mountain's large stones. Then he freezes, stunned by the scene that greets him. It looks to his young eye as though the armies of Rome have descended upon this garden and its olive press.

Before him are several hundred Roman soldiers. There are also temple guards, servants from the high priest's house, and dozens more who form what can only be described as a mob. They carry lanterns, torches, swords, and clubs. Some of the lanterns hang from long poles. The mob brought these expecting they would have to search the notoriously dark, rugged face of the mountain. They came expecting a manhunt for a rabbi on the run.

Each piece of the mystifying scene sears itself into the boy's mind. Jesus stands calm and regal before the officers. His clothes are wet with a rust-colored liquid. Some of his men are nearby, looking scared, resigned, perhaps embarrassed. The rabbi's other men stand a bit further away, terrified and confused. There is a figure the boy recognizes as the high priest's steward. He is well known in the city. The steward is to the side of the crowd and appears deeply shaken. From time to time he puts his hand to his ear and feels it eagerly. Then there is the great mass of armed men who crouch slightly, their weapons stretched before them, as though making themselves ready to repel an invasion. But there is no obvious threat beyond the few old swords the boy knows that some of the disciples have tucked in their sashes. Something yet unseen has filled these men with alarm.

The boy would learn later what had happened in the moments before he arrived. Jesus and his men had come to the olive press garden to pray. It had been a fairly pleasant evening. They had partaken of the feast in the second-story room of the house in the Upper City. There was tension, particularly when Judas became offended and left, but they had enjoyed the start of their walk toward the garden in the refreshingly cold night air.

Then things started unraveling. While they were still making their way, Jesus said solemnly that they would all be offended and flee from him that evening. Some said it wouldn't happen. The rabbi stood his ground and shot back that it would not just happen once but one of them would betray him three times. Shame and hurt fell over them. How could it be? One of them angrily insisted the rabbi was wrong this time. It was quiet for a moment. When they arrived at the garden, Jesus took three of them some distance further to pray.

What followed was embarrassing. While Jesus seemed to be in a state of prayerful agony, moaning and yelling as though giving birth, the rest could not stay awake. The food, the wine, their general sadness at the evening's decline and the lateness of the hour all conspired against them. Jesus asked three different times that they stir themselves and help him watch, but they couldn't. They slept. They awoke in guilt. Then they slept again.

Finally, they awoke to hear Jesus say something about the hour being upon them and his betrayer approaching. This was startling enough to jerk them out of their slumber. When they stood and looked about them, they were surrounded by hundreds of armed men, a few temple officials and, of all people, one of their own—Judas.

In a loud, unnatural voice, Judas shouted a greeting to the rabbi and then kissed him, not once but over and over again. Jesus did not answer this feigned affection. "Judas," he asked, "you betray the Son of Man with a kiss?" This was rhetorical. Jesus didn't wait for an answer but instead stepped past Judas toward the bulk of the armed men.

"Who do you seek?" he asked evenly.

"Jesus the Nazarene," someone of rank said.

"I am he," he replied calmly.

At this, the armed men drew back and toppled over. It would have occasioned a laugh had anyone dared. When the soldiers recovered themselves, the rabbi asked the same question again.

"Who is it you want?"

Again: "Jesus of Nazareth."

"I told you I am he. If you are looking for me, then let these men go." It was not so much a request as a command. And it came after a demonstration of authority. The soldiers were unable to stand when this rabbi declared himself. Surely they understood that if he did not choose to be taken, he would not be. *So, let the others go*, he urged. *There is something inevitable happening here and we should get on with it.*

Armed men then grabbed him and started to bind his hands. His men saw this and became incensed. One of them pulled his sword, swung it at the high priest's steward, and sliced off the man's ear. The armed men gasped, gripped their weapons tighter, and moved forward. Jesus spoke to the man who swung his sword before he could do further damage. The armed men stopped in their tracks. "Put your sword away. Shouldn't I drink the cup the Father has for me?"

"The cup." In all of their holy writings, a cup that was not for drinking natural liquid was a cup symbolizing God's wrath. Perhaps some begin to understand.

The rabbi bent down, picked up the bloody ear, and put it where it belonged at the side of the servant's head. When he took his hand away, the ear remained in its place, attached and undamaged as though it had never been severed. The servant, whose name was Malchus, moved unsteadily aside.

The boy has hardly moved since he came upon this scene. He remains frozen still, as burly men grip the bound rabbi and move him down the mountain. The hundreds of others, having found what they came to find, also begin moving toward the Valley of Kidron and head toward the city.

It slowly dawns on the young man that dozens of the armed men in this seething mob are passing within a few feet of him. The realization comes to him just in time. Several soldiers step in his direction to grab him. He jumps back. The men end up with fistfuls of cloth. The boy spins and dodges, coming free from his sheets.

He runs away, naked, the taunts of the men in his ears as he goes.

Now, completely exposed, he must find his way back down the mountain, across the valley, and into the city. He must do this without being arrested. He feels the shame of his situation and it becomes one with the shame of all who have run from the side of the rabbi this night.

The shivering, terrified boy suddenly realizes what the others already have: Jesus—their rabbi—is about to die.

Vindicta:
THE VENGEANCE

House of Caiaphas
Jerusalem
14th of Nisan, 3790

It might have entered his mind. If it didn't, it is certainly under-standable.

He had spent tortured hours in prayer earlier this night, while his men slept the sleep that comes after food and wine. Nothing he could say would rouse them. He was agonizing alone, even bleeding into his sweat, when a mob closed in. The mob's leader was one of his own, the kind of man willing to cover his rabbi with kisses to mark him for death. Then there was that moment when he granted a glimpse of his power, after soldiers asked about Jesus of Nazareth and he said, "I am he." They stepped back in fear and fell to the ground. Had he not held himself in check, all of them might have been flung from the mountain. He also healed the ear of the high priest's servant after one of his men foolishly drew his sword, and he kept from harm everyone who had been entrusted to him. In return, each of them ran, leaving him alone before his enemies.

It had already been a long night. He might not have given it thought.

The soldiers tied his hands and moved him roughly down the mountain. They followed more or less the same path he had taken five days before, when he rode the unridden colt westward into the Holy City and a great throng cheered him. He is cheered now by no one and walks only with men who want to see him die.

So when he reached the bottom of the valley and they pushed him across the bridge, the sound of rushing waters below him in the cold, did it enter his mind that the brook Kidron ran red? Did he think for a moment about the blood and the filth of the temple sacrifices? Did he recall just then that for years the priests poured into this stream all that remained after the rest was offered to God? Did it come back to him that he, too, was a sacrifice and that like this meager stream that rose to a torrent in winter, he would bleed into the land after all else had been given? He had said as much before. Did these certainties live in him as he crossed the bloodred brook at the bottom of the gorge?

Perhaps the thought of the Kidron gave him comfort. Sacrifices ascend to someone. Perhaps it was this thought that stilled him on that night: when the day of evil was over, he would rise. It is what sacrifices are meant to do.

They took him across the swirling red waters, then, and up the incline on the other side. They turned slightly to the south. Finally, there were stone steps and he climbed while they pushed and shouted. At the top was a house protected by a broad courtyard and eager servants. Fires burned here and there and people gathered tightly around them in hopes of burning away the cold.

He knew the place. It was the high priest's house. But they weren't taking him to Caiaphas. They were taking him to Caiaphas's father-in-law, Annas, the former high priest, now ruler of the temple markets.

It signaled everything to come. It was late in the night. He had been arrested by hundreds of armed men, most of them Roman. Yet they did not take him to the Praetorium or to the Fortress of Antonia. They brought him here, to the high priest's house. Even then, they did not take him to the ruling high priest. They took him to Annas, who had no authority over him but insisted upon seeing the one who caused him so much trouble. This told Jesus all he needed to know. The law would not be observed. This was personal. What lay ahead was Annas and his vengeful schemes.

•◄▐▬▬▬

When the time comes, soldiers shove him through the door of the house, wind through several of its rooms, and stop before a seventy-year-old man. The two eye each other. Annas, ever cool and precise, speaks first. The guards remain at Jesus' side.

Annas asks first about the men who follow Jesus. This is a taunt. Here before Annas is one who speaks to thousands from mountainsides and who was nearly carried into the city by masses of pilgrims at the start of the week. As a man much impressed with power, Annas took note.

Now, though, this self-proclaimed king is bound and alone. Annas had heard from his guards and his servants this evening, perhaps also from Malchus of the severed ear, how the men with Jesus had run. Annas delighted in the snide tale about the naked boy who scampered into the night. *What happened, rabbi?* He did not need the information to help him arrest these men. That would not be difficult for a man with Annas' network of spies. No, what he wants is a moment to gloat. The enemy who has eluded

114

capture for so long is here—and no one comes to his aid. *Tell me, rabbi, where are these men who hold you in such esteem? Not one is devoted enough to stand by you?*

While Jesus stands, his hands tied tightly behind him, and Annas sits, smooth and mockingly polite, the questions turn to teaching. He has no intention of learning from Jesus. He is a Sadducee. There is nothing a Sadducee does not know. He probes. He feigns interest. He turns a phrase over and asks for explanation. This goes on for quite some time. Finally, Jesus is no longer willing to accommodate the game. There are laws.

"I have spoken openly to the world. I always taught in the synagogues or at the temple, where all the Jews come together. I said nothing in secret. Why question me? Ask those who heard me. Surely they know what I said."

Jesus is not asking why Annas does not have better information. He is appealing to the mandate of the Sanhedrin's own laws. He is being detained, even bound. He has not yet been charged. Instead, Annas probes for something he can make into a crime. It is backward. Charges come first, on the testimony of two witnesses. Then the questions. But it transgresses the laws of God and man to use the latter in hopes of finding the first.

What you are asking about is already known. I've hidden nothing. Please, bring out your case.

One of the guards thinks this is insolence and strikes Jesus on his face. For a Jew, it is a shattering insult. It is a violation and it is cowardly. Strike a bound man? Again, it signals what is coming. This is the first of many blows Jesus will receive, and not one of them will be justified under the law.

"If I said something wrong, testify as to what is wrong. But if I spoke the truth, why did you strike me?"

There is no answer. Annas is bound by nothing. He owes this rabbi no explanation. He is accountable to neither man nor principle. He is the ruler of this land. Kings and priests do his bidding, and he intends to make this Jesus pay. The law is a thing one uses to achieve ends. Jesus has cost him. This is what he knows. He will do as he pleases, and he is pleased to end this man's life.

Both men see this for what it is. The meeting comes to an end.

Soldiers shove Jesus from Annas' presence and take him to the sitting high priest. Caiaphas is waiting—elsewhere in the same house—and he is not alone. With him is nearly every authority in the nation: the chief priests, the Sanhedrin minus a few, the elders and the teachers of the law. They have been waiting. They are eager to bring this matter to a close.

As had happened before with Annas, the meeting does not begin with charges of wrongdoing, though it is the only legal way and what God requires. Instead there are only questions. Jesus says nothing. He sees what this has become. It is useless to give an answer. Let them play this out if they can. The God of Israel is watching.

Witnesses who have been well prepared give testimony, but their accusations are so confused it is obvious they lie. Even the most creative mind can find no basis for a charge. Frustration rises. Men glare accusingly at each other. There has been great effort to bring this moment about. Surely, after all that was required to arrest this man, they will not fail to even make a case.

More witnesses testify. There is nothing of substance. It is late. This gathering is tiresome and there is danger that Rome looks on. Perhaps now new testimony can bring this meeting to a close. Finally, desperate, officials shove new witnesses forward. There is some eagerness, even excitement.

It is not to be. These new witnesses make a tired claim: *he has called for the destruction of the temple and promised to rebuild it in three days.*

There is squirming. Priests look to each other uncomfortably. For some, it is humiliating just to be in the room, so pitiful are these proceedings. Conspirators though they are, brilliant men are here. They can detect lies, discern character. They have spent their lives judging facts. They cannot be treated as fools. They know the difference between a truly treasonous act and a poetic, symbolic statement used to persuade in a speech. No one genuinely believes Jesus has made such a claim. He might be deceived but he is not insane. Only a madman would claim to build the temple in three days. It is the best they have to work with though, and Caiaphas, mortified by how the night is unfolding, works to incite the rabbi in some way he can use.

Jesus says nothing. These men are condemning themselves. Caiaphas senses it also. He is jaded but he is no fool. He launches into a frantic performance.

"Are you not going to answer?" His voice is filled with mock pleading.

Again, Jesus does not speak. He is not obligated to under the law. There have been no charges. There is nothing to answer. And tonight, in this evil affair, there is simply no purpose.

Caiaphas presses: "What is this testimony that these men are bringing against you?"

There are eminent jurists in the room but their gifts are not needed to know this is a mistake. The high priest should not ask the accused to explain testimony against him. It exposes the weakness of his case. It makes his sidestepping of the law obvious. It allows the accused to win sympathy. No one could answer such a question. The room fills with embarrassment at what this has become.

Caiaphas knows he must redirect. "Are you the Christ, the Son of the Blessed One?"

Jesus need not answer. There is nothing about this gathering that is just. The law that should govern this moment, holy to a Jew as little else, is cast aside by the very men the nation looks to for justice. There are no charges. There are only questions in search of a charge. The meeting is at night and takes place in a private home. It does not convene at "the chamber of hewn stone" in the temple where the Sanhedrin is bound to meet. It follows an arrest arranged by "blood money." Each of these is a serious, punishable transgression. In this room, each of these is ignored.

Lies prevail, but the larger issue has become perfectly clear. The conspiracy to murder Jesus has moved unwittingly into the light. It is the almost perfect creation of the House of Hanan, the perverse dynasty of Annas.

It is established. This proceeding has made it so. The law of

God no longer rules in Israel. Nor, in the minds of these men, does God himself. This gathering is the evidence. Israel is ruled by thugs. Power has replaced righteousness and profit is its purpose. There is no reason to think otherwise. There is now no difference between Jerusalem and Rome.

No one is more certain of this than Jesus. He has been declaring it for years. In fact, this is precisely what has brought him to this moment. These men intend to put him to death. There is no law, no custom, and no allegiance that can dissuade them. They rule unrestrained.

Caiaphas is waiting. He has asked if Jesus is the Christ, the son of the Blessed One. He pauses. The rulers of Israel hope this is the turn.

"I am." Two words. A statement of truth. In a house of lies, it stuns. Jesus is not finished. "And you will see the Son of Man sitting at the right hand of the Mighty One and coming on the clouds of heaven."

This is what Caiaphas has been waiting for. He tears his clothes. It is an official act. Blasphemy is present. A desecration has occurred. All must come to a stop until this wicked act is cleansed from the land.

A high priest tearing his garments is meant to be a sign of

grief. It is what righteous men do when the holy is touched by the unclean, when the character of God is assailed. Had grief filled these men in Caiaphas' house, had they wept and agonized at what a false prophet claimed—fallen to their knees and begged for mercy from an offended God—it might have hinted at true holiness among at least a few of the men in this room. It might have offered some evidence that they are more than criminals in robes.

Yet there is no grief. There is no repentance, no pleading with God for the nation. Instead, the leaders of Israel conduct themselves like mercenaries in a rage. They shout that Jesus must die. It is what they hoped for when they first conspired. Now, they spit upon him and blindfold him and command him to prophesy. They are relieved that the case is closed and furious at what this man has said. They strike him. They curse him. They do nothing different from what the criminals of Rome would do.

The meeting concludes. Men congratulate themselves upon their success. They will see this man die yet. Tomorrow, they will enlist the aid of Pilate. For the rest of the night, Jesus is locked in the jail beneath the high priest's house.

It is 3:00 a.m. on the 15th of Nisan in the year 3790. And Israel is dying.

XIV

Judicium:
THE JUDGMENT

The Praetorium
Jerusalem
The 15th of Nisan
7:30 a.m.

So the clash of gods has come. Pilate had hoped it would. He had been told what was taking place on the far side of the city when he and his men entered Jerusalem on the first day of the feast. It was pitiful. A country rabbi rode a colt into the city, having traveled all of two miles. He was celebrated only by pilgrims who happened by.

What did it prove? Why the concern? One rabbi. One colt. Some tree branches. Some pilgrims with nothing to do.

By the way the leading Jews reacted, it might as well have been a Persian invasion.

Pilate had ridden sixty miles with hundreds of men and enough seasoned warriors to destroy all of Judea. These Jews could certainly twist themselves into knots over nothing. He would never understand.

He has just received word that Caiaphas and the Sanhedrin are coming to him for affirmation of their ruling. They arrested this Christus just last night. One of the man's followers gave him up for a few coins and they found the rabbi hiding among olive trees low on the mountain across the Kidron. The Jews asked Pilate for troops to support their temple guard. He sent several hundred. It was over in a few hours. He's been told that the Sanhedrin met late into the night, that they interrogated the rebel, beat him, and ruled that he's a threat. Early this morning, they met again and decided to deliver him up. Pilate had hoped he would not have to get involved. It is not to be.

The Jewish delegation arrives at the Praetorium with Jesus in tow. He is bound and badly beaten. It does not begin well. This is a holy day to the Jews, their Passover.

They must be particularly careful not to become ceremonially unclean. If they do, it will mean they cannot partake of the feast of their god. To even enter a Roman's house—a house with the exotic reputation of Herod's Palace in particular—would mean exclusion from Passover.

It is all so tiresome. The governor must leave the palace and judge the matter from an elevation of rock outside. He would not do it had the emperor not begun to soften on the Jews. Tiberius commanded his governors to do likewise. Pilate already has political problems in Rome. He does not need enraged Hebrews suggesting to the emperor that the governor of Judea is anything but compliant.

He hopes to make quick work of this. He seats himself, sees that a crowd is gathering—he suspects they are curious about the rabbi—and sternly demands a report.

"What charges are you bringing against this man?"

"We have found this man subverting our nation. He opposes payment of taxes to Caesar and claims to be Christ, a king."

The words are too well chosen. The clerics would turn him against this man. Pilate will not be so easily controlled.

"Take him yourselves and judge by your own law."

"But we have no right to execute anyone." Good. A start. *We want this man dead and we want you to do it. You've stripped us of that power.*

Pilate wishes to investigate. He knows it cannot be done in front of this delegation. He rises from his seat and walks back into the Praetorium. No Jew will follow him. He sends for Jesus.

When the prisoner arrives, Pilate can see nothing threatening.

He already suspects that this man is guilty of no more than getting in the way of Annas' ambitions. It is an old story.

"Are you the king of the Jews?" This is Roman bluntness. He has little patience for verbal gymnastics.

"Yes, it is as you say." The rabbi speaks plainly, too. It is a rare trait in Jerusalem.

Pilate waits. Silence. Under Roman law, the accused must make a case in his own defense. If he remains silent, his guilt is assumed and sentence is passed. Pilate waits for the impassioned speech. Nothing comes.

He wonders if the man understands this. The chief priests have made numerous accusations against him. To say nothing is to guarantee death.

"Aren't you going to answer? See how many things they are accusing you of?"

Silence. Pilate tries once more. "Are you the king of the Jews?"

Jesus speaks. "Is that your own idea, or did others talk to you about me?" It is a matter of importance. *Are you asking this of me as a Roman? Is this your own idea? If so, you are asking if I am a rebel. Or, did someone talk to you about me? Then it was likely a fellow Jew, and what they have told you is that I think I am the Messiah.*

The answer disturbs Pilate. He hears the insinuation that he is not his own man, that he does the bidding of the chief priests mindlessly.

"Am I a Jew?" Pilate asks. This comes in bitter tones. "It was your people and your chief priests who handed you over to me. What is it you have done?"

"My kingdom is not of this world. If it were, my servants would fight to prevent my arrest by the Jews. But now my kingdom is from another place." Jesus will not be lured into defending himself. Instead, he declares his kingship in different terms.

Ah. The clash of the gods. Pilate knew it would come. "You are a king then!"

"You are right in saying I am a king." How unusual this man is to speak so simply, in such certain terms. "In fact, for this reason I was born and for this reason I came into the world, to testify to the truth. Everyone on the side of truth listens to me."

"What is truth?" The rabbi touches the anger, perhaps the disappointment, in Pilate's life.

There is weariness in this. The governor is a man with no faith beyond the one imposed upon him: divinity of the state. He lives in an empire that makes every new god its own, that absorbs nations by absorbing their deities. It has made Rome a roiling religious sea—a god for every occasion, an altar for every need, and a priest ever demanding offering. Pilate has seen a man kneel at an altar on the street and beg to be heard though he does not know which of the many gods to invoke. *It is a travesty. Which petty deity rules a journey on water? Is it the same god for rivers as for lakes? For lakes as for seas? How horrible that a man might die because he cannot keep track. And this Jew speaks of truth. There is no truth. There are only truths. Even they are fictions.*

The rabbi may be a fanatic, but the man has done nothing to deserve death.

The governor returns to the raised stone of judgment. Again, he takes his seat. The crowd has waited. They grow silent, eager. The delegation of priests looks nervously on. What has transpired inside?

Raising his hand as a sign of authority, Pilate declares, "I find no basis for a charge against him." The people shout. The priests plead. Then one of their voices rises above the noise. "He stirs up the people all over Judea by his teaching! He started in Galilee and has come all the way here!"

Pilate has not heard this before and now he sees the path. *So, he is a Galilean?* The Jews confirm this, but they see their mistake. Their case is slipping from their hands.

It is Pilate's deliverance. *If this man has come from Galilee, then he is under Herod's jurisdiction. Perfect. Herod has come to Jerusalem to sacrifice in the temple. He has already been here three days. Let him decide the case of this Jesus.*

Word reaches Herod Antipas, who could not be more delighted with this opportunity. He has attended closely to the news of Jesus, though he is still uncertain as to who the man is. Is he Yochanan, the baptizer, come back from the dead? Is he Elijah? Perhaps one of the other prophets? Herod is fascinated with this rabbi's magic and hopes to see him do something thrilling. He is also pleased by the opportunity to end tensions with Pilate. The two have long been at odds. *Send the rabbi.*

The interrogation by Herod is nearly a riot. Jesus will not speak, Herod demands some astonishing sign, and the chief priests and teachers shout their accusations. No one can be heard. It is chaos. Finally, in frustration, Herod and his soldiers taunt Jesus and mock him by dressing him in an elegant robe. *If this Galilean will presume to be a king, we will give him garments equal to his station.* Like his father, Herod the Great, Herod the son fears the rise of a true and destined king of Israel. He knows he reigns merely at the pleasure of Rome.

Herod returns the prisoner to Pilate. This cooperation eases feelings between the two officials and, in time, their friendship is restored.

Pilate wishes to bring the matter to an end. He summons the priests. "You brought me this man as one who was inciting the people to rebellion. I have examined him in your presence and have found no basis for your charges against him. Neither has Herod, for he sent him back to us, as you can see. The man has done nothing to deserve death. Therefore, I will punish him, and then release him . . . It is your custom for me to release to you one prisoner at the time of the Passover. Do you want me to release the 'king of the Jews'?"

The priests were prepared for this. Pilate can shed blood without a thought but he will seldom take a righteous stand. It is no surprise he offers the Passover pardon. It frees him from the burden of decision.

They have schooled the people, though, and at the signal they begin to chant. "No! No! Not him. Give us Bar Abbas."

Pilate is dismayed. This Bar Abbas is a murderer. He's clearly an enemy of the state. The people, however, have been stirred by their priests. Now, Bar Abbas must be freed.

Still, there is the issue of this Jesus. Perhaps there is yet some room to maneuver. There is a tactic Pilate has used before. He will scourge this unspeaking rabbi. If Pilate's experience is any guide, the rabbi will emerge so hideous it will wring pity from the masses. The Sanhedrin will lose their control over the crowd and then perhaps Pilate can let this Christus go.

XV

Excoriare:

THE TORTURE

The Praetorium
Jerusalem
The 15th of Nisan
Approximately 8:00 a.m.

It is cowardice that moves Pontius Pilate to order this scourging. The Prefect has not even rendered a judgment in the matter of the Galilean rabbi, but still he orders the cruelest form of punishment possible shy of death under Roman law. Fear fills him. Fear of Caesar. Fear of the Sanhedrin. Fear of the people. He will give the screaming masses a bloody spectacle whether they want it or not. What he will not do is free this man. It would cost him too much. He cannot allow it—though he has already declared the man innocent.

For Pilate, this rabbi is a political problem. For his legionnaires, the man is an object of snarling hatred. *He is one of those arrogant, idiotic Jews. He thinks he is a king and that God has chosen him personally to rule. There is only one God who lives in the only true temple—the one in Jerusalem. This fool has even called the temple "my house." What a disgusting piece of filth he is. He thinks he is some kind of god and yet here his own people have betrayed him into the hands of Rome.*

His people! The "Chosen People"! How the Jews insist upon such words. But they are a small, divided, conquered tribe. They would not even have a temple if it weren't for the generosity of Rome. Yet their leaders think themselves so much superior that this morning they refused to enter the Praetorium for fear of being tainted. Rome is to be spat upon in this way? Rome is this "unclean"? Let this deceitful rabbi feel the wrath of "unclean Rome"!

It is a scourging Pilate wants. He needs blood on display. Those who heard him order it and who think he means something like the usual "whipping" are unfamiliar with Roman ways. This is a scourge, what the Romans call "the halfway death." Its purpose is not to slice into a man for a while so he remembers not to disobey. No, a scourging is how Rome strategically flays a man so he is never whole again, how it rips flesh from bone.

The soldiers act immediately. As soon as Pilate gives the order, they take the prisoner into the Praetorium. *Now, the arrogant Jew belongs to us.* Out of public view and with only their comrades to impress, they prepare to unload their rage.

At the order of an officer, guards shove Yeshua into a court-yard. They remove his clothes, thrust him against an upright post, and tie his hands to a ring that hangs above his head. This stretches the muscles of his arms, back, and shoulders, positioning them perfectly for what is about to come.

The work of scourging is done by a *lictor*. He has been care-fully trained. There is an art to this, for the Roman scourge is more than a matter of blunt force and rage. It is a matter of expert use of the *flagellum*, one of the most effective instruments of tor-ture ever devised. Simple, ingenious, and cruel, this flagellum is a ring of iron or wood to which leather straps are attached. What makes the flagellum so horrific are the bits of sheep bone, rock, or steel knotted into each leather strand.

Yeshua's hands are tied so that he is just able to stand on his own. Then comes the first strike of the flagellum. It is devastating. The lictor does not slap the leather against his victim. Instead, he swings the flagellum so as to partially wrap its straps around the victim's torso. Then, once the jagged bits in the leather have bitten into flesh, the lictor yanks the flagellum in reverse. Skin tears. Blood gushes. Pieces of muscle and sinew, even chips of bone, fly into the air. The body is torn apart. This is the purpose of scourging: to break a man, to shred him, to make him less than whole.

With the second strike, Jesus can no longer stand. He is hanging from his hands, too stunned and weak to find his feet. The strikes come more rapidly. He does not have time to think. His mind blurs. Each knotted strap is like a gnarled claw ripping away fistfuls of flesh.

A red spray hazes the air. Dozens of tiny pieces of the prisoner are flung about the floor. The lictor himself is sheathed, shiny and wet, in the victim's blood. It is a badge of honor within his trade. After dozens of strikes, Yeshua's back, arms, chest, buttocks, and upper legs are shredded. They look as though they have just been plowed. Strips of flesh hang loosely, barely attached at one end.

The Jews insist upon limits to such tortures. Their Law forbids more than forty lashes. The priests allow no more than thirty-nine lashes in case the lictor miscounts. This, of course, has led to much debate. And absurdity. One rabbi has insisted that floggings should be stopped only when males soil themselves with excrement and women soil themselves with urine.

None of this matters now. It is the Romans who are scourging Jesus and they have no such scruples. They scourge until the victim passes out. Then, they splash the offender with water and wait for him to revive. When he does, they scourge him more. It is why this is called the "almost death." The lictors are proud of their trade and observe exacting standards. The soldiers who look on appreciate the bloody distraction. They know nothing of craft and standards and art. They enjoy the sport and the gore.

There is another brutal fact that adds to this heartless treatment. The men scourging Jesus are soldiers in the Roman army, but very few of them are Roman. Most of Pilate's troops are local. It is the same with armies of occupation everywhere, for it is always cheaper to fill the ranks with auxiliaries from nearby than with costly troops from home. This is why most Roman troops in Jerusalem are not Romans but Samaritans and Syrians. They are mercenaries. They care little about Rome or the honor of Caesar. What they do care about is their hatred for Jews. This means that Jesus is being scourged by men who despise him for his race, who want him to suffer horribly just for being a Jew. It makes an already bloody form of torture into a racist slaughter visited on one man.

Jesus has gone limp. He seems to be dead. The lictor looks to the ranking officer for the signal to stop. It comes. This scourging has been savage. Some of the bones in Jesus' back are exposed. He has lost vast amounts of blood. His flesh is shredded as though a wild animal had been gnawing on him. He is ghastly to look at, nauseating, even for those who have seen a scourging before.

Pilate will be pleased. The prisoner's appearance is so horrifying that, surely, the people will see he has suffered enough already and should not be put to death.

Jesus is untied from the ring atop the upright pole. He immediately falls to the ground. Guards drag him harshly to his feet and hold him up so that the gathered warriors can have a look. Soldiers grunt their satisfaction. He is almost dead though not quite. It is perfect. The lictor has done well. His comrades honor him and shake his hand.

The soldiers are not done, though. There is fun yet to be had. Since the prisoner claims to be a king, the soldiers intend to give him the homage he is due and in a style he will never forget. They summon the rest of their company and dozens more assemble. Word of the amusing farce spreads. Quickly, someone finds an old *sagum*, the purple robe worn by an officer. It is perfect. Someone else twists thorn branches into a crown, making sure the unusually long spikes turn inward to better pierce the brow. When it is finished, it looks like a sadistic version of the laurel wreath a Caesar wears. A reed serves as a scepter and once it is positioned on the prisoner along with the robe and the crown, the game begins.

The robe and reed are mere symbols meant for humiliation. The wreath of thorns, though, is a continuation of the torture. Its spears are inches long and the man who places it on the criminal's head presses firmly until most of the thorns have pierced the skin. Profuse bleeding begins. Blood pools in the eyes and the ears and then dries. It flows down upon his neck and shoulders, blending with the blood already oozing from dozens of other wounds.

The soldiers circle their dying prey. They laugh at the worthless Jew in his comically regal clothes and begin performing a perverted version of the homage paid to a king. "Hail, King of the Jews," they shout, over and over again. They bow and chant and stand at full attention as if Tiberius Caesar stood in front of them. They roar their laughter to urge each other and then begin chanting again.

In time, this loses its appeal and the blows begin. Yeshua has been struck already today by one of the temple guards. That was long ago, before the scourging. It was nothing compared to a blow from a Roman soldier. These men train for years in hand-to-hand combat. Their lives sometimes depend upon delivering jaw-crushing blows. Their experience shows as they repeatedly strike the grisly-looking, disoriented Jew from the direction he least expects.

Before long one of the soldiers picks up a staff and uses it instead of his fists. Swinging the weapon in great arcs, he brings it down powerfully upon the criminal's head, stunning the man with its force. This continues, blow after blow: first the wooden staff and then the fists. The soldiers can taste the bitterness of their hatred in the back of their mouths, much as they do during a battle. They sense energy flowing through them. Some are surprised at how it drives them against this one insignificant man.

They spit upon the Jew, mocking the kisses offered to an emperor, and continue to bow and chant his name facetiously. Strangely, after all his tortures, the prisoner is still standing. The soldiers beat him with the reed meant to symbolize his scepter. *Some king he is. A mere blow with a reed causes this man to shudder.*

An officer calls for the prisoner to return to Gabbatha, the pavement stone where Pilate sits waiting outside. The soldiers enjoy one final insult, a last blow with fist or staff. Then they end their game. It is time to appear respectable. They wipe blood from their hands and faces, adjust gear, and straighten themselves as befits Caesar's men. They must not appear to be thugs. They form around the bloody ghost and prepare to appear before Pilate.

The prisoner is now nearly unrecognizable. Until he moves in some small way, it is hard to tell whether he is alive or merely balanced upright by the guards. He does not look human. He looks freshly returned from the dead.

This, of course, is just what Pontius Pilate wishes.

Crucio:

THE CRUCIFIXION

The Praetorium
Jerusalem
The 15th of Nisan
Approximately 8:30 a.m.

Pilate emerges from the inner rooms of the Praetorium and stands once again upon the raised pavement outside. He takes in the growing crowd before him. He is hopeful. This Jesus of Nazareth who has caused so much trouble and whom the Jews wish dead has just been scourged. Pilate expects the man to look like all the other flagellum victims he has seen. He knows well what his men can do. Perhaps this will appease the Jews and their leaders. Perhaps they will be horrified enough to let the matter of this rabbi rest.

Pilate senses the dramatic opportunity of the moment. "Look!" he shouts, gesturing grandly: "I am bringing him out to you." He allows these words to hover before he says more. And then, "I find no basis for a charge against him."

On cue, the soldiers shove Yeshua into the sunlight. Great gasps of horror arise from the crowd. The man they want killed hardly looks like a man at all.

He is wearing the purple robe of high-ranking military men. There is a woven wreath of thorn branches sitting low upon his head. Thick, drying, dark-red blood covers him completely. Where the tattered robe hangs open, the crowd sees what the thunderous work of the lictor has done. The man's chest is mashed, red skin. On one side of his torso, the distinctive shape of his rib bones protrudes. His face is badly swollen and each step he takes causes such spasms that some in the crowd have to look away.

Then, Pilate: "Behold, the man."

After the gasps of horror subside, there is no sound as the people take in what the flagellum has done. Disgust and awe register on faces. The chief priests and temple officials begin to panic. They know this stunned silence is their enemy. They cannot give the people time to contemplate this man's suffering. They take up their chant: "Crucify him! Crucify him!" Their agents in the crowd do likewise. Soon, the people shake loose from their stunned grief at Yeshua's appearance and start to remember what a blasphemer he is. Now they too shout and pump their fists.

"You take him then!" This is Pilate in disgust. "I find no basis for a charge against him."

The Jewish leaders are ready for this. They have no intention of letting the Roman slither out of the dilemma they have fashioned for him. "We have a law, and according to that law he must die, because he claimed to be the Son of God."

Pilate has not heard it this way before. He knew the Galilean claimed to do miracles and thought himself a king. He also knew that the man stormed about the temple as though it were his personal domain. But Pilate had not been told that this man claimed to be the Son of God. This means he is issuing a direct challenge to Caesar. It changes everything.

Straining to hide the terror in his face, Pilate returns to the safety of the Praetorium's inner courts. The guards push Yeshua after him. Once inside, the Prefect rages.

"Where do you come from?" He is shouting. There is no answer.

"Do you refuse to speak to me?" The governor is nearly screeching in his frustration and fear. There is no reply.

"Don't you realize I have power either to free you or to crucify you?" Pilate finds it difficult to sound threatening just now.

Through the radiating torment of his shattered body, Yeshua replies evenly: "You would have no power over me if it were not given you from above. Therefore the one who handed me over to you is guilty of a greater sin."

This undoes Pilate. The calm, measured manner of this dying rabbi already haunts him. There is no fear in this bleeding Jew—not of death nor of pain nor of those with power.

The Prefect walks slowly, hesitantly, outside again and begins to plead. The priests, the people, other Roman officials, even Pilate's own guard stare back at him astonished. The man who walks as Caesar in this land is humiliating himself, pleading with worthless provincials so they do not force his hand. It is embarrassing. Guards look away in disgust.

The scribes and chief priests are prepared. They know the phrase that will make the already nervous Prefect shudder. "If you let this man go," they shout, "you are no friend of Caesar! Anyone who claims to be a king opposes Caesar!"

The words penetrate. Emperor Tiberius is a notoriously suspicious man. He would entertain the whisperings of influential Jews. How could Pilate explain how he freed a man who thought himself the emperor's rival? These Jews have made themselves into Caesar's protectors. It is genius.

Pilate knows these words for what they are: the unanswerable threat. He is resigned. He walks again to the stone pavement before the palace and lowers himself into the judge's seat.

Gesturing weakly toward the prisoner, he offers, "Here is your king."

"Take him away!" comes the chant. "Take him away. Crucify him!"

"Shall I crucify your king?" Pilate asks the crowd.

"We have no king but Caesar," the priests and people declare.

Pilate knows the Jewish leaders have sold their souls for this man's death. There is nothing more to do. He surrenders the prisoner to be crucified.

"Crucify him! Crucify him!"

The angry palace crowd demands crucifixion. They want the blasphemous rabbi killed. Their leaders stir them, otherwise they might remember what crucifixion is. They might remind each other that crucifixion is a public torture meant for the living. It is a curse of fear, a spirit of terror unleashed upon the land. It is designed for killing a man, certainly, but only by way of killing a people's spirit.

It was not originally something Jews would do. Believing that the human body is made in the image of God, Jews would not execute a man in a way that violates his body. It is why murder is outlawed and ritually cutting the skin in grief is forbidden. Even tattoos are a sin. The body must be kept whole and unmarred, as near to the purity of creation as possible. To deform a human body, or to defile it as crucifixion does, is prohibited.

Of course, one Maccabean ruler, King Jannaeus, set aside these restrictions and crucified more than eight hundred people in the Holy City itself. This was not so long ago. Thankfully, it was an exception.

Most Jews find crucifixion revolting and believe it to be against the will of their God. Their own authorities execute by strangulation, beheading, and stoning. They sometimes hang criminals too, but only those guilty of idolatry or blasphemy and only after they are dead. The hanging of a dead body is meant as a lesson to the living. Hanging is never used to kill. In fact, the Law of God gives such fierce warnings about defiling the land by hanging a man improperly that the authorities seldom order it: "When someone is convicted of a crime punishable by death and is executed, and you hang him on a tree, his corpse must not remain all night upon the tree; you shall bury him that same day, for anyone hung on a tree is under God's curse. You must not defile the land that the LORD your God is giving you for possession."

This same law causes Jews to view capital punishment as a sacred duty rather than an act of human vengeance. The Sanhedrin even fasts on the day they vote in a matter of execution. They would not call for a man's death without asking the guidance of God. Thankfully, death sentences are rare. It is possible for a man to serve in the Sanhedrin his entire life and never rule upon a single sentence of death, so hesitant are the Jews to offend their God by withholding mercy or giving in to vengeance.

When a sentence of death has to be issued, stoning is the preferred method of execution. This takes place at the *Beth haSequilah.* According to law, the first witness shoves the condemned man from an eleven-foot-high elevation. If the victim survives this, the second witness hurls a large rock at his heart. If death still has not come, all the witnesses and bystanders stone the guilty one until he dies.

It is a priestly act. It is meant to cleanse the land of sin, atone for offenses, and remove anything that might make a holy God abandon his people. To do otherwise is to risk too much. Sin must be judged, the stain upon the land expunged. Righteousness demands it. So does survival.

This is how Jews understood execution and how they traditionally carried it out—until Rome ended Israel's authority to put criminals to death. Now, Israel must appeal to Rome to execute the lawless, and Rome executes by crucifixion.

In the Roman mind, crucifixion is an act of state terror. It is a method by which one man is so excruciatingly and horribly put to death that all who see it cower. The Romans did not create the science of crucifixion, but once they learned it and refined it, they made it serve their purpose. For Caesar's legions, crucifixion is an art of empire.

No one is certain whether the practice began with the Persians or, like much else in the world, the Phoenicians. The Assyrians, Scythians, and Thracians each had their versions of it. Once Alexander the Great saw its power, he used it to horrifying effect. Thousands were crucified at his command. It was Alexander, in turn, who introduced crucifixion to the Romans and they transformed it into a weapon for subjugating nations.

What each of these nations wanted was a method of killing that leads to more than just death. Most of them tried impaling, boiling, burning, stoning, strangling, and drowning their victims but found them all too quick. They wanted a way of killing that was slow and terrifying enough to make sure that no onlooker could miss the intended threat. Crucifixion served perfectly.

It is ingeniously simple. To be crucified is to be "staked." Its purpose is not death but—as the Latin name for the practice suggests—*cruciare*: torture. It is the ideal combination of death, vengeance, spectacle, and terror. It is perfect for the needs of imperial Rome, which experimented with crucifixion for decades before arriving at the most satisfying approach.

It is the impaling of a man that turns execution into crucifixion. He can be impaled to a tree, a hillside, even a wall. It doesn't matter. Some societies have executed their enemies by impaling them to the crossbeams of their own houses. The goal is always the same: kill a man slowly while keeping him in place and causing him unspeakable pain.

Originally the Romans impaled the victim's feet and tied the hands with ropes. This proved inefficient. The victim lived too long, sometimes up to a week, so guards had to stand watch when they were more urgently needed elsewhere. Further experiments surfaced a solution: impale both the hands and the feet. This increased the victim's suffering, guaranteed a more entertaining spectacle, and usually assured death in no more than a few days.

The Romans also noticed the inadvertent tortures of crucifixion. Their executioners knew that stripping victims humiliated them and subjected them to the cold. They did not understand at first that public nakedness is shameful to Jews, but it took them little time to make this part of the sport of killing as well. In Israel, the chief priests pled for the use of a loincloth.

Nature adds to the agonies the condemned endure. Insects, birds, and even rodents pick at the flesh. The sun glares. Wind, rain, and snow often play a role. The impaled man can do nothing to stop these agonies. The gathering crowd taunts. The victim's relatives must helplessly watch it all. Always there is the stigma of crucifixion. It was originally intended only for the lowest of men. The universal command that begins a crucifixion is *Pone crucem servo*—"put the cross upon the slave."

The Romans have, over time, developed precision in their approach. They know just how high to make the *stipes crucis*, the upright beam that rises from the ground, so that a ladder is not required to mount the victim. They know just how long to make the *patibulum*, the crossbeam, so that the condemned can carry it and soldiers do not find it too heavy to lift once a human body is impaled. Even soldiers new to execution know how many men are needed to stake a man and then stand guard, how many hammer blows it should take to drive in the stakes and how best to speed the process of death. They are efficient. A hundred years ago, when Spartacus led his rebellion of slaves, the empire crucified six thousand men in a single day. For weeks afterward, the birds and insects picked at bodies lining the road from Capua to Rome. Veterans still remind recruits of the glory of those days.

The veterans also tell stories of the sport that accompanies crucifying. They gamble for the victim's few possessions and mock the dying to entertain the crowds. They get creative about the impaling. Sometimes they drive spikes through victim's ears or joints. When a criminal particularly angers soldiers—perhaps because he wronged a beloved commander's daughter or stole from a legionnaire—they think nothing of driving a spike through the man's penis or scrotum, even through his tongue. Any variation is permitted as long as the feet and hands are impaled and death does not come too quickly.

What the crowd at the Praetorium forgets in its rage is that crucifixion does not just remove the threat of one man. It makes whole nations into whimpering sheep. It is meant to rob the spirit that could cause people to resist or rebel.

The Jewish leaders congratulate themselves. They have moved Rome to kill an insurgent rabbi. They tell themselves they have won a great victory this day. In truth, they have merely helped Rome further demean the people of Israel.

Lamenta:
THE WEEPING

Jerusalem
Praetorium to Golgotha
The 15th of Nisan
8:30 a.m.

The sentence of death has been issued. Pilate has used his *ius gladii* as Annas and Caiaphas knew he would. The man simply had to be shown the price of indecision. It helps that Pilate is petrified of Rome.

Now things happen quickly. Pilate steps to a large bowl of water on a high stand tended by a servant holding a towel. He begins to wash his hands. As he does, he turns to the crowd with an almost threatening look on his face. *This deed is not on my head. I am free of this man's blood.* The governor knows what he is doing. He has been among Jews long enough to understand the meaning of hand washing at such a time. It is described in the Jews' own

Torah and means that the one washing is free of "the guilt of shedding innocent blood." It is what Pilate now declares before all.

The crowd, incited by their leaders, has been chanting. As Pilate dips his hands a last time into the water, their words seem more relevant than before. "His blood is on us and on our children!" they shout.

As Pilate returns slowly to the palace, a centurion begins giving commands. He orders the purple robe removed from the prisoner. He assures that the loincloth is secure and that the prisoner's hands are tied with sufficient space between them. He has done this before and knows that for the prisoner to carry the patibulum, his arms must be able to form a larger opening than is possible if his wrists are tightly tied.

The centurion sends guards to retrieve two prisoners who will also be executed this day and he dispatches other men to bring back three of the "trees." This is the soldier's word for the patibulum—the crossbeam that the three prisoners will carry to the place of execution.

Pilate had been specific about the wording of the *titulus*, the white wooden board that announces the crimes of the condemned. Soldiers carry one ahead of each prisoner during the procession to Golgotha and then nail it above the victim's head after he is impaled.

It forms a kind of epitaph over the man's life. Pilate has ordered that the rabbi's titulus read, *Iesus Nazarenus Rex Iudaeorum*: "Jesus of Nazareth, King of the Jews." The members of the Sanhedrin objected. They wanted the words changed to "*He said he was* king of the Jews." It seemed more the description of a crime and less the granting of a title. Pilate was unmoved, still resenting these men for playing the crowd—and even Caesar—against him. "I have written what I have written," he replied: *Quod scripsi, scripsi.*

The centurion barks the formation into order. A cavalryman rides at the front. His horse helps to part the crowds and his mounted height helps to announce the spectacle of crucifixion. Three soldiers abreast follow this rider with still others forming behind them on each side. This creates a type of box around the prisoners, which keeps them from escaping and, in cases of particularly despised criminals, keeps the crowd from killing the condemned before the proper time. Within this box are the three condemned men with a soldier who carries the titulus just before each.

It is time for the procession to begin. At the centurion's command, men not part of the formation lift a patibulum onto each prisoner's shoulder. These crossbeams are roughly cut and weigh seventy-five pounds. It is a mercy. If condemned men were required to carry the entire weight of the cross on which they will die—

both the patibulum and the upright stipes crucis—it would weigh more than three hundred pounds. Most would never be able to do it. They would either die from the beating the soldiers would mete out in punishment or they would die of the strain of trying to carry such a load. This is not the Romans' plan. They want the prisoner to live now so he can die later in a far more horrible way.

The order is given and the detail advances. The destination is Golgotha, a quarry/cemetery outside the city walls where Rome executes its enemies and its lawless. The unusual name is an Aramaic word that means "place of the skull." This is both because Golgotha is an outcropping of rock that looks like a skull and because the skulls of the dead cover the ground. The site is well chosen. It has the virtue of being close to Herod's palace where sentencing takes place and it is also near a city gate. The soldiers who must marshal beaten prisoners the entire way are grateful for the short distance.

The procession moves slowly. Two of the prisoners have not been scourged. Jesus, though, looks as though he has been mauled. He stumbles often and recovers slowly, leaving bloody marks along the road. From the Praetorium in the Upper City and through the neighborhoods nearby, the criminals and soldiers together arduously climb hills and pass through narrow streets.

The centurion quickly becomes frustrated with the slow pace. The entire distance from Herod's palace to Golgotha is less than seven hundred feet, and it should not take this long. They are still shy of the city gate. Just then, the centurion notices a man walking through that gate from the opposite direction. Since it is accepted tradition and established law that a Roman officer may command any service from any civilian at any time, the centurion orders this traveler to carry the prisoner's patibulum. The conscript's name is Simon. He is from Cyrene but has just come from the nearby countryside. He is eager to get about his business, but Golgotha is only a few hundred feet away and this intrusive assignment should not take long. More important, he has no choice. The centurion has commanded. He grips the seventy-five-pound crossbeam, hoists it to his shoulder, and walks within the box of guards at Yeshua's side. The centurion is pleased. The usual pace resumes.

It is a feast day and so shops and markets are closed. Still, the curious come to see and then, as word spreads, a crowd forms. Women begin to weep. Some know this struggling, bleeding prisoner is the controversial Galilean rabbi. Others are simply moved by the sight of a viciously scourged man. The grief grows and some of the men looking on join the women in their weeping. The crowd is undone. Soon, there is a wave of anguish and wailing.

This summons something in Jesus and he begins to speak. It surprises the soldiers and quiets the throng.

Daughters of Jerusalem, do not weep for me. Weep for yourselves and for your children. For the time will come when you will say, "Blessed are the childless women, the wombs that never bore and the breast that never nursed!" *Then,* "they will say to the mountains, 'Fall on us!' and to the hills, 'Cover us!' For if people do these things when the tree is green, what will happen when it is dry?"

Now, as Yeshua leaves the city, he repeats the dire prophecy he gave as he entered days before. *Destruction is coming. Jerusalem is unaware. Women will wish they had never brought children into the world.*

Soldiers at Golgotha see Yeshua coming and continue the mocking from earlier in the day, the mocking that attended the savage scourging. They offer the parched prisoner a cup of wine mixed with myrrh. He refuses. The soldiers do not intend this as help, as a sedative to ease his pain. They are still mocking him for claiming to be a king. Wine with myrrh is a delicacy. Kings drink it. The wine and myrrh are one with the tattered purple robe, the reed scepter, and the twisted crown of thorns.

When the prisoner is six feet from the stipes crucis reserved for him, the march ends.

Would that the prisoner's sufferings were at an end. Would that a skillful slitting of the throat or a knife from behind at the base of the skull or a sword swung in a great arc to sever the head or a spear through the heart brought the sufferings of three decades and the torment of recent hours to completion.

What came next was none of these: nothing so merciful or quick, nothing so humane. What came next was the Roman Empire's precise procedure for public and excruciating death. Yeshua had already endured more than most men of his or any age. He had not yet endured enough.

Iniuria:

THE INJUSTICE

Golgotha
West of Jerusalem
The 15th of Nisan
9:00 a.m.

The work to be done at Golgotha is routine. The Roman detail assigned to this duty have performed their tasks many times. There is no thought to a man's life ending. There is no grief, no revulsion at the anguish and the gore. Only enemies and criminals are sentenced to die in such a manner. The more of them dispatched the better.

Yeshua has barely obeyed the order to halt when a soldier takes the patibulum from Simon of Cyrene and throws it to the ground. A second soldier roughly grabs Yeshua and throws him backward. His shoulders land heavily on the rough, splintered wood of the crossbeam. This opens the wounds on his back and blood seeps into the wood and the soil.

It is not the first time today this has happened. After the scourging, the soldiers put that old officer's robe around him. Dried blood adhered its broken fibers to his wounds. When it was yanked off of him at the Praetorium before the procession through the city, his wounds tore open and bled. It weakened him further and made him unable to carry the patibulum beyond the city gates.

His body is moved harshly with kicks and shoves to align it with the beam. Once in place, the most experienced among the executioners takes three spikes in hand. They are iron and tapered, measuring five to seven inches in length. They have been used before. Skillfully, the soldier uses a mallet to drive the spikes into Yeshua's arm.

The Romans had learned through much trial and error. It would not do to impale a man through his palms. The flesh between the bones of the hand is too soft and tears easily, particularly on a larger man. It wastes time. Soldiers on crucifixion details learned to drive the spikes into the wrist.

While one man holds Yeshua's arm to the beam, the more senior man feels for the depression in his wrists. He finds it, knows to position the spike just above, and then, hammer in hand, drives the spike into the wood with a surprisingly few number of blows.

The procedure is repeated for the other arm. The soldiers

know that the condemned usually feel the first pangs of panic at this moment. They are lying on the ground impaled to a beam they cannot lift. They realize this is how they will die.

Once Yeshua's arms are impaled, four soldiers position themselves along the beam—two next to his torso and two on the opposite side. They firmly grip the beam, and then at a signal they lift the patibulum with the prisoner attached and hold both high in the air. Carefully so as to not lose balance, they walk the beam to the upright stipes crucis and lower it down upon the very top, where a mortised slot has been prepared. The wood now makes the shape of a *T*, the prisoner hanging limply from it.

Quickly the soldiers bend the prisoner's knees, which allows them to flatten his feet one over the other against the upright beam of the cross. Again, the experienced executioner takes over. Feeling for the space between the second and third toes and then moving his hand to the very top of the foot, he finds the proper spot and drives a spike through both feet that penetrates through to the wood.

Yeshua's arms are spread and impaled to the patibulum. His knees are together and turned to one side. His feet are nailed one on top of the other. He is not stretched out or elongated to his full height. Instead, he is crouched slightly, as though in a partial squat.

The last task for the soldiers is to position the titulus. The Romans have learned to crucify their victims low to the ground. To impale the victim at a height means far more exertion, much climbing of ladders and unstable lifting of bodies and wood. Yeshua is impaled in such a way that he is barely two feet above the ground. It makes the work easier, faster. Rome has been known to crucify thousands of victims in a single day. It is only possible if the work is reduced to a minimum effort, if every step is economical and efficient. The titulus, then, is attached with little trouble.

That the titulus is inscribed in three languages—Greek, Latin, and Aramaic—is demanded by the location of Golgotha. The rock hill of execution sits beside a great road that leads from Jerusalem to the north. On this day in particular, thousands will travel this road. Though it is a Jewish feast day, it is not a Sabbath and travel is not restricted. Jews from throughout the empire and foreigners of every kind will happen by.

Once the initial work of crucifixion is done, the soldiers quickly turn to sport. They cast lots for the prisoner's clothes. It is sometimes the last thing the dying man sees: executioners gambling for the few possessions he leaves in this world. There is cursing and laughter. Men shout with glee when the lot falls their way and at other times scuffle and argue over the loot.

Just as his own garments are dispersing into the world he leaves behind, Yeshua speaks for the first time since being impaled.

"Father, forgive them; for they know not what they do."

Already he is experiencing the dark secret of crucifixion. From the moment the spikes pierced his wrists, great bolts of pain began shooting through his arms. This pain has intensified and spread. Now, Yeshua's forearms knot and cramp, the searing agony moving into his upper arms and shoulders. It is constant, wracking, unspeakable pain.

This, though, is not the hidden horror of crucifixion that so delights the Romans. Once a victim is impaled, he quickly realizes that if he hangs from the spikes in his wrists, his pectoral muscles paralyze. It means he can take air in but he cannot exhale. With his lungs full yet unable to breathe out, he panics. This registers on his face and in his twitching and spasms. His executioners have waited for this moment and they howl at the sadistic entertainment.

The prisoner soon realizes that the only way to keep from suffocating is to push down on the spike through his feet. This lifts him up to relieve the stress on his arms. It is an unspeakably torturous move. It rotates his forearms around the spike in his wrists, scrapes his back over the jagged wood of the stipes, and grips his legs in agonizing cramps. It eases him slightly, though, by allowing him to breathe. He cannot hold the position long. Soon, he finds that pressing down on the spike through his feet is so exhausting that he has to lower himself and hang from his wrists again. Until the panic returns. Then, the sadistic cycle repeats. In the barracks, grizzled legionnaires call this "the dance of death."

The representatives of the Sanhedrin have seen this "dance" before and choose this moment to begin their taunting. They speak to Jesus but intend their words for the crowd. "He saved others; let him save himself if he is God's Messiah, the Chosen One." The soldiers know this as a signal and begin their taunting too. "If you are the king of the Jews, save yourself."

One of the criminals dying at his side mocks him also. "Aren't you the Messiah? Save yourself and us!" The other dying man summons the strength to answer: "Don't you fear God, since you are under the same sentence? We are punished justly, for we are getting what our deeds deserve. But this man has done nothing wrong."

Nothing is said for many minutes. There is only the sound of desperate breathing, of grunts and gasps and straining men. The second criminal speaks. He has been thinking, has found a bit of courage. He pleads: "Jesus, remember me when you come into your kingdom." He did not get this idea of who Jesus is during the events of the day. He has heard the rabbi speak before. It did not keep the criminal from his lawlessness, but what he has heard brings faith now. Then Jesus speaks.

"I'm telling you, this same day you are going to be with me in paradise."

There is silence, broken only by the sounds of the "dance of death." For long periods, Yeshua's chin rests on his chest. His arms tremble involuntarily. He shakes like a man freezing to death and yet this shaking comes from within—from lack of air, the trauma of the scourging, and the crushing strain in his limbs. Just when onlookers might think he is dead, he jerks harshly from a shock of pain. Realizing he is suffocating, he pushes upward in near panic until he can exhale and breathe again. The agony of it all registers on his face, and in the blood falling in great drops to the ground and in the flesh torn from his back by the rough crossbeam each time he moves.

It is just at such a moment, when he has pushed himself up on his wounded feet to breathe and can turn his head to look, that he sees her. She has not been near during much of the day and though he was glad she did not see his suffering, he wondered if she was safe. Now, she is standing just beyond the slope of the rock hill where he is dying. One of her son's men has brought her, knowing there isn't much time.

XIX

Damnatus:
THE CONDEMNED

Golgotha
The 15th of Nisan
Noon to 3:00 p.m.

He can see in his mother's eyes that she does not understand. She never really has and she has said as much. It didn't help that she was told more than anyone except the son who hangs before her dying. No mother could understand this.

Oddly, it was that she didn't understand but was willing to believe anyway that allowed it all to begin. She was barely a decade and a half old when the visitor appeared. He said high and beautiful things. What she heard with certainty was that she was about to have a child. She asked the natural question—natural for her years, natural for the explanations she would be forced to give, and natural given what was about to happen to her body. "How will this be," she said, "since I am a virgin?"

There was no resistance or disbelief in this. Just the need to know. The visitor explained. *You will be overshadowed by God. That is why the child will be called the son of God. Here, I'll give you a sign. Your barren cousin, Elizabeth, is about to have a child. You can be sure, no word God speaks will fail.*

Mary clung to the phrase she needed most: "No word God speaks will fail."

Then, let it be to me according to that unfailing word. It was how she surrendered. She did not think she was really supposed to understand.

It occurred to her later that demanding to understand first would have been a mistake. Zechariah, her cousin's husband, proved this. While he was doing his priestly duty in the temple, the same messenger who spoke to Mary suddenly appeared. He announced that Zechariah's aging wife would have a child and that the boy would set things right for the Messiah.

Zechariah didn't collapse in joy or begin worshipping the God whose presence was just beyond the next curtain. Instead, he asked, "How can I be sure of this?"

The messenger felt no need to explain himself. He declared that his name was Gabriel and that he had come from his post in the presence of God to deliver the good news. Since Zechariah demanded understanding but refused to believe, he would be struck dumb until the child was born.

Nine months later Zechariah's son, Yochanan, came into the world. Mary gave birth six months later. She never did understand how it had all happened, but she was willing to believe it would.

It was never easy and this is why thirty years later she needed a sign. She saw it, in those six huge water jars at Cana. She also needed his attention from time to time but there was usually someone demanding a word or a crowd pressing around him. She worried it was all affecting him, even the state of his mind, and that's why when it once became too much she told her children to rescue him.

Years before she had been warned of the pain she would endure: "And a sword will pierce your own soul too." She couldn't have been prepared. It had been hard to see how badly he had been treated through the years, but it was also hard to be treated harshly by him. He was speaking to people in a house once and all she wanted was to be with him. It was her right. She is his mother. She sent someone to give him the message that his mother and brothers waited outside. He wouldn't leave what he was doing. Instead, he told the crowd that everyone who does God's will is his mother or his brother.

Really? Then let them bear what she has borne. Let them earn the right.

The disappointment, hurt, and unanswered questions fixed themselves in the air between them. Until this moment.

She has just arrived at Golgotha and she is holding on to a friend's arm so she doesn't collapse from the ghastly scene before her. Around her are some of her family—those not too fearful to come—and it is good that they are here because they would not have believed it if she had told them.

Her son. The promise. The one God gave her . . . in every way. Pieces have been torn from him. Great gashes expose his bones. There are holes in him. He is dying because he cannot breathe.

Grief and guilt and an aching need to hold her son well up in her. There is anger too. Where are his brothers and sisters? James, Joses, Judas, and Simon. Are they still afraid? After all this time, don't they believe? Or do they need further proof? Whatever it is, they are not here. Their brother is bleeding to death alone.

He sees her now. She is certain. With enormous effort, he rises, breathes, and speaks. "Woman," he says hoarsely, tenderly, "here is your son." He makes the slightest movement of his head toward his closest friend. Fixing his eyes upon the man, he says, "Here is your mother."

John stares. He understands. He waits a moment for Mary to absorb and then squeezes her arm and turns her gently toward the road. It is not a request. She will not see the end. It is what Jesus wants.

Once again, Mary must acquiesce without understanding. Once again, she does as is required against every strand of her nature. The sword predicted so many years ago pierces deeply.

●◄▬▬▬

Her leaving would tear the heart from his chest were it not that after she is gone the world goes dark. It is only noon. He has been impaled for three hours. Something, and not just darkness ruling the sky, has changed.

The Sanhedrin members who taunt from the edge of the hill grow quiet to ponder what this means. Priests look up from their Passover preparations, the temple guard tenses, and even the Romans wonder which god is at play.

The Jewish leaders know what such things usually mean but surely, they hope, not on this day. For in all the literature of the law, the prophets, and the histories of God, when heavenly bodies fail—when stars collapse and moons go out and suns cease to give light—it is a prophetic, poetic statement that kingdoms will soon fall. The Torah says that the sun, moon, and stars were put in the heavens to govern. They have become symbols of rulers and government and kings. Moons go black and suns leave the sky and stars fall to the ground in the language of prophets to signal that God is moving against nations.

It is a sign of judgment upon this deceived rabbi and his followers, the priests tell each other. *It can have no other meaning.*

This darkening of the heavens has meant a change in Jesus. Already his agonies have nearly overwhelmed him, but they are mostly physical. Something inside is tormenting now. His body is wracked with the ravages of his scourging and impalement but his soul seems to be elsewhere. It too is tormented and yet not by matters of steel, wood, or stone.

Not long after the sky blackens and Jesus begins wrestling with something unseen, the horrible cry fills the air. It is eerie and low at first but then it rises and haunts the hearers the rest of the day. It is the screaming of the lambs.

This is the Day of Preparation and in these next hours the sacrificial lambs will be slaughtered. Already men have been carrying their white, bleating offerings to the temple. The killings begin at three.

It counts as one of the great religious feats of mankind. At the appointed time, each male Israelite carries his lamb into the temple courts. There, he will slit the lamb's throat and flay it while a priest collects the blood in a sacred basin. The priest will pass the basin to other priests, much as men pass buckets of water to extinguish a fire, until it reaches the last priest, who stands before the altar. That priest splashes the blood in the basin against the altar steps. While this is done, the man making sacrifice remains in an outer court. He must peel the lamb's skin from its flesh and remove the entrails, which are then sent to the altar for burning. All the while, Levites play musical instruments and chant or sing the Psalms.

The noise of it all is deafening, but it is due mainly to the lambs. Once the slaughters begin, the lambs begin to scream. They hear the cries of other lambs being sacrificed and they can smell the stench of blood, which first reaches them outside of the temple. In the court—which is only 230 by 66 feet—bodies cram together. Knives flash and blood spews. Hides pile up on the floor and dung is thick and pungent. Most men find it a siege of the senses. It is no wonder the lambs scream.

The number of sacrifices is difficult to imagine. A lamb is offered for every family. As many as 150,000 people are present. That means nearly five thousand lambs are sacrificed, or forty-two lambs a minute during the two hours allotted for the offerings on the Day of Preparation.

Those two hours are rapidly approaching.

Jesus has entered the extreme edge of human suffering. He has lived through the "almost death" of the scourging and then the beating by the soldiers. The arduous walk from the Praetorium to Golgotha followed. That was five hours ago. Since then, he has been impaled on a Roman "tree" while religious men mock him and passersby applaud his "dance of death." Joint-twisting cramps plague him. He is suffocating most of the time. Tissue peels from his back every time he moves. He hardly looks human. And there is a new horror: a deep, crushing pain in his chest. His heart is surrendering to his tortures. Death is close.

His cousin the baptizer told everyone he could that Jesus was the "Lamb of God, who takes away the sin of the world." If it is true, then that sin is upon him now. Perhaps it is why he seems inwardly removed; why, since the darkness of noon, his agonies press more deeply into his soul. If he is enduring the world's evil, as his cousin taught that he would, then perhaps the vileness and filth of humanity is besetting him now. It may be the worst of what he has withstood.

The afternoon drags past its midpoint. The sky is still strangely dark and the air is growing cold. The women who have followed Jesus and cared for his needs since Galilee stand at a distance. There is Mary Magdalene, James' mother who is also called Mary, and her sister, Salome. There are others and they keep an appropriate distance so as not to draw the attention of the soldiers or the priests, but they weep and wish they could care for Jesus now.

Then comes a loud, grief-filled voice. It is Jesus. No one would have thought such a force could come from a man who looks as monstrous as he does. He has pushed himself up once more for air and then shouted, *"Eloi, Eloi, lama sabachthani?"* It is Aramaic and it means, "My God, my God, why have you forsaken me?" It is haunting, this sound, filled with despair and the alienation of a man abandoned by God.

Some think he has called for Elijah. To their ears, he has: the Aramaic word *Eloi* is the same as the Hebrew word for *Elijah.* They shout at him, thinking him mad. That he speaks in Aramaic makes the soldiers stop their distractions and look at him. Troops from Italy would have understood nothing he has said, but Samaritans and Syrians from nearby know Aramaic. These mercenaries have understood, have heard this man's agony in terms they know.

In moments more, he moans, "I thirst." Someone quickly

offers a sponge soaked in *posca*, the vinegar wine of the Roman soldier. He drinks it.

The wine does not refresh him but seems to signal a completion, a release of some kind.

"It is finished," he proclaims weakly but as though he is commanding it to be done.

Then, in that otherworldly voice that has come from him just moments before, he shouts, "Father, into your hands I commit my spirit."

It is more than a shout. It is a scream, really. And since it is three in the afternoon on the Day of Preparation, his scream blends with the screaming of the lambs.

And he is gone.

Centurio:
THE CENTURION

Golgotha
Friday, 7 April
784 AUC
3:00 p.m

It is the centurion who first declares it though others in the crowd should have. There are priests walking by constantly and members of the Sanhedrin nervously looking on. Teachers and scribes are everywhere. So there were many who should have understood what it all meant before a foreigner did. The priests and the scribes are supposed to be guardians of the land and the law, the advocates of truth. This foreigner, the centurion, is commander of a hundred or so mercenaries, but he had the courage to say it out loud and he risked his life to do it.

He has good reason. The man whose titulus reads "King of the Jews" had just shouted out his last breath. He had pushed himself up to get a last gulp of air and then he screamed—it was more of an anguished roar, really—"It is finished. Father, into your hands I commit my spirit."

It was the man's death cry. Anyone who heard it knew that something was different about this particular ending of a life. And it didn't take much knowledge of the Jewish law and prophets to see the importance of what happened next: an earthquake. The shaking knocked stones from buildings and walls, split the ground, and even spilled open tombs. It was unsettling, even for a battle-hardened centurion, and the fact that it has been dark since noon already made the day unsettling.

It must have struck the centurion like a blow from one of the Roman siege engines. He had seen the prisoner tried, scourged, harried through the streets of Jerusalem, and tortured by impalement for six hours. Seconds after he died, the centurion knew. Maybe it came in the terror of the earthquake. Or from the rumors: people leaving the city reported that the massive temple curtain had torn in two. Maybe it was simply the sound, the man's voice as he forced out his last words.

"Surely, this man was the son of God."

Those were the centurion's words. He wasn't paying a compliment. He wasn't cravenly trying to appease a god. He was declaring of Jesus what he had often been required to declare of the emperor. This man is the *divi filius.* It was the Latin title of the great Emperor Augustus. It means "the son of God." The centurion was changing religions. He was leaving the worship of Caesar and devoting himself to this criminal Jew.

People heard. Some joined him in giving praise to this God and some beat their chests in anguish. Others walked away angry. It will get back to the centurion's commander, even to the governor, Pontius Pilate. The members of the Sanhedrin who are still here will make sure of it. There will be consequences.

●━◀▌▬▬▬

In the dark, then, as the dust settles from the earthquake and minds reel from the final cry of the prisoner and the astonishing confession of the centurion—as priests watch from the edge of the little rock hill of crucifixion and weeping women look on from further away and the soldiers begin thinking they've killed a deity—the chief priests do a typically odd thing. Someone tells the centurion and he prepares to obey, but the strangeness of the order occurs to him.

These chief priests. There is no understanding it. They take this Jesus to Pilate because they want the man killed. They've trumped up charges and everyone knows it. But they won't walk onto the pavement around Pilate's house because it will make them ceremonially unclean! Then, they have no problem seeing this man tortured to death all day but they can't have his mangled body hanging up past sunset the night before their holy day.

Word has come from Pilate that the bodies are to be removed. The chief priests have requested it so that there is no religious contamination. It is the law of Rome, and Pilate will comply. The passage from the *Digesta*, the summary of Roman law, is well known.

The bodies of those who are condemned to death should not be refused their relatives; and the Divine Augustus, in the Tenth Book of his *Life*, said that this rule had been observed. At the present, the bodies of those who have been punished are only buried when this has been requested and permission granted; and sometimes it is not permitted, especially where persons have been convicted of high treason.

The bodies of persons who have been punished should be given to whoever requests them for the purpose of burial.

It is a mercy from Rome but in this case it means killing men first.

The prisoner called "King of the Jews" is already dead. He was scourged before he was impaled. In fact, he was certain to die after the scourging alone. It just took six hours for him to do it. The other two prisoners were not scourged and though they suffer the agonies of patibulum and stipes, they can live on many hours, perhaps even days more.

Unless something is done. And it will be. The chief priests have requested it.

The centurion nods to his men. One of the soldiers walks a short distance away and retrieves a board. It is about an inch by three inches wide and about four feet long. It is for administering the *crurifragium* and it comes with a steely logic. These prisoners are only alive because they can still push themselves up to breathe. Keep them from breathing and they die. This means breaking their legs. The *crurifragium.*

A soldier moves to one of the living prisoners. Broadening his stance slightly, he swings the four-foot club at full strength into the impaled man's lower leg. The bone cracks. The man screams. Another swing and the other leg breaks. The man sinks down as far as his pinned arms allow. He cannot rise again, so he cannot breathe. Within minutes he is dead.

The soldiers turn to the "King of the Jews." He seems to be

dead but when men on this detail have misjudged death before they have paid for it. Better to be sure. Grabbing his spear at mid-shaft, one of the mercenaries thrusts it into the side of the dead man, somewhere between the fifth and sixth ribs. No response. When the soldier pulls the spear out, what looks like blood and water pour out. John, Jesus' friend, sees this. He had taken Mary to his house earlier, as Jesus wished, but now he has returned. He will tell often of the blood and the water that flowed from his friend's side. Satisfied, the centurion's men turn to the third pris-oner and dispatch him with two blows of their wooden club.

The work is done. The prisoners are dead. The small crowd that remains starts to drift away. The Sanhedrin members who have hawked over every moment of the proceedings now scurry back through the Gennath Gate and to the temple to join the Passover preparations. The screaming of the lambs grows louder.

The centurion and his men need only gather their gear and report their assignment done. But the centurion himself is changed. He has seen the man he now believes to be the son of God and he has said so before witnesses. It is treason and he knows his commander will hear of it. Dishonor and perhaps even death may await him. He did far more than simply declare that the Gali-lean rabbi, not Tiberius, is the son of God. He found joy in it. A witness will later report that after the darkness of noon and the earthquake at three followed by the death cry of the prisoner, the centurion "praised God." Whatever comes next for him, his life will never be the same.

Excessum:
THE DEPARTURE

Near the Gennath Gate
The 15th of Nisan, 3790
3:00 to 5:00 p.m.

The centurion is not the only one to risk much now that Jesus is dead. While at Golgotha some who knew Jesus and loved him hover about—a few standing guard against the birds and the flesh-eating pests—a man some distance away moves boldly to bring this day to a proper close. It could cost him his life.

His name is Joseph. He is important because he is a member of the ruling council of the Jews, the Sanhedrin. He's not an insider, though. He hasn't ingratiated himself to Annas to put money in his pocket or rise to power. In fact, he's a secret follower of Jesus who has not said so publicly because of his fears.

This fear is hard to understand. Joseph, a Jew and a powerful man, is afraid of the Jews, so he does not tell other Jews that he follows a Jew. There must be two types of Jews, then. There is the Jew who is Jewish because he believes and keeps the Law. This is Joseph, certainly. Then, there are "the Jews" who are the upper crust of Jewish leaders. "The Jews" appointed by Rome. "The Jews" who control trade for their families. "The Jews" who serve a man named Annas. Political Jews. Public Jews. Official Jews. Not all of them men of genuine faith. Not men who hope for the coming of the Kingdom of God, the appearing of the Messiah, or the consolation of Israel.

Joseph is a believing Jew. It is why the message of Jesus, who wanted not to destroy the Law but to restore it, appealed to him so much. And even though he is a member of the council and a man due respect, he is wary of "the Jews," who always hated Jesus and conspired from the first to kill him. Annas rules "the Jews" along with his son-in-law Caiaphas, and Joseph has been careful to stay out of their way. He did not want to be crushed by Annas' political machine. In turn, Annas and "the Jews" usually ignore Joseph. It is the reason they did not bother to involve him in the council's decision to execute Jesus. Joseph likely would not have joined them if they had. He is afraid. It is tragic. A Jew afraid of "the Jews."

Until now. Today, he has seen too much and is beyond disgust. "The Jews" took over and manipulated the Romans into murdering a man who had done nothing deserving of death. And they didn't just stab him in the night or engineer an accident. "The Jews" broke their own laws to try the man, have him scourged and then impaled. It has been a sinful affair.

Joseph is fed up. He surprises almost everyone by going "boldly" to Pilate. "Boldly." It's what a witness later said. No one in the council would have described Joseph as bold. Things have changed. He asks Pilate for the body of the Galilean executed today. Pilate agrees. He knows the law and, besides, doesn't care who buries the bodies of criminals. It gets the Sanhedrin off his back. They want the man buried by sundown. What is it to Pilate who does the work?

It does not escape the governor's notice that the nobleman asking for the body is a member of the council. *So there are followers of this Jesus on the ruling council.* Things are not as he was told.

Joseph has declared himself a follower of Jesus. Why else would he want the body? It won't be long before everyone knows. The men on the streets of the city. The priests at the temple. The rest of the Sanhedrin. Caiaphas. And, of course, Annas, who has probably already been informed by his spies.

Joseph's indignation has driven away his fear. Rushing from his meeting with Pilate at the Praetorium, he turns toward Golgotha.

The body must be prepared and it must be done by sundown. There is very little time. Thankfully, Nicodemus joins him. This is a surprise. He may have known that Nicodemus—also a member of the Sanhedrin—met with Jesus once in secret, but he could not have known that Nicodemus would help him with this heartrending work. Soon, the whole city will know.

The men hurry out the gate and on to Golgotha. It is cold and dark. The wind rises. The rock of Golgotha seems somehow colder still. Few of those present during the day remain. The women are there—still weeping, still eager to tend their master, still keeping themselves at the appropriate distance. John too is there. He cannot pull himself away. Others walk by on the road, hurrying to finish their business before sunset—though it will be hard to determine just when that is, given the darkness of the sky since noon. Arriving travelers notice something happening on the little rock hill and can just discern in the dark that a small group of men are removing a body.

Perhaps no one at Golgotha notices who is missing. The business of burying Jesus is left to two members of the Jewish ruling council with permission from the Roman governor. But where are Jesus' men? Where is the one who promised to lay down his life? Where is the one eager to die with Lazarus? He is of little help to him who raised Lazarus. Where are the rest of Jesus' men? And where are his brothers and sisters? He is left to men who barely knew him—and a handful of faithful women.

It is good that these women are some distance away from where Jesus is impaled and that Mary is not here. Removing a dead body after a Roman crucifixion is not a pleasant task. Joseph and Nicodemus, along with a few others whom they have asked to help, work to pull the spike from the overlaid feet. The legs barely move. The muscles have grown rigid from their trauma. The men lift the patibulum off of the stipes crucis and lay Jesus upon the ground, still attached to the crossbeam. They pull the spikes from his wrists. The hours of hanging from the wood have pulled Jesus into a nearly inhuman form. His limbs have to be forced. It is ugly and adds to the deepening grief.

The men move Jesus to a flat area of rock and begin to clean him. Beyond cleaning his face, hands, and legs, there is little they can do. They have sent for linen, and Nicodemus, who knew what was needed, brought anointing compounds. In fact, he has brought an amount appropriate for royalty—seventy-five pounds of aloes and myrrh. For the moment, they wrap the body with a linen cloth.

Though Joseph is from Arimathea, he has decided to make

Jerusalem his home. It is the reason he purchased a tomb for him-self. Fortunately, it is not far from where they are. He offers it. They lift the body and carry it quickly in that direction. There is little time for discussion.

Everything now is hurried. They take the body to the tomb and set it down in the courtyard just before the entrance. They tear strips of linen and begin wrapping the body further, infusing ointments between the layers of linen. They push the mouth closed just before they cover the eyes and wrap the head. It is a rushed job. They have no choice. Perhaps they can return after the Sabbath and finish the work.

The sun is setting—strangely, in the darkness. The men enter the tomb and light lamps in order to see. They lay the body on the limestone shelf, infuse the strips of linen with more ointments and then pause. The women are looking on.

A final ritual is required, now that everything else is done. By tradition, a feather is placed under the nose of the deceased. Attendants are expected to wait fifteen minutes. If the feather moves, the man is still alive, if only barely. If it is still, the soul has left its earthly home.

The men place the feather and sit quietly in the flickering

light. They can feel their weariness. Their thoughts run over the evils of the day. They wait.

The feather does not move. It is over. They knew it was.

They tamp out the lamps, take a last look, roll the large stone meant for covering the door into place, and urge each other to the city.

EPILOGUE

In approximately 30 AD by the Gregorian calendar, 784 by the Roman calendar, and 3790 by the Hebrew calendar, Jesus was brutally killed. Only a few holdouts dispute this.

Yet what that death meant, if anything, will be disputed until the end of time.

It seems that something of importance did happen two days after Joseph of Arimathea and Nicodemus put Jesus in a tomb. We can be forgiven if we are unsure about all the details. Even those who followed Jesus and watched him die were confused. Decades later, they still had not come up with an official version of the story.

John, the only writer of a gospel who was actually there, wrote that on the Sunday morning in question, one woman named Mary Magdalene went to the tomb in the dark and found the stone door moved. She hurries back into town to find the cowardly Peter and the author, John, who describes himself as "the beloved disciple." He and Peter run to the tomb and John is careful to tell us that he gets there first. He hesitates, though, and Peter brushes by. Inside, they find the burial linens carefully folded but no Jesus. Both men go home. Mary Magdalene sits in the cemetery weeping and then goes back to the tomb and finds two angels sitting where Jesus' head and feet had been. They ask her why she is crying. She says she can't find Jesus and then someone appears behind her. She thinks it's the gardener. It isn't. It's Jesus. He tells her to tell his men, who are somewhere in hiding, that he is no longer dead.

It is a very human and very tender—even humorous—conclusion to an anguishing few days. Most of us would be satisfied if this was the only version handed down through the years. It would give us much to think about, perhaps much to live for.

But there are four gospel writers, and the other three don't agree with John.

Mark, whom scholars believe got his details from Peter, has three women going to the tomb. Again, the stone at the entryway is moved. They enter the tomb, find a young man who announces Jesus is "risen," and he instructs them to tell his "disciples and Peter" that he has gone north to Galilee. The women flee, trembling and in terror. They then tell—absolutely no one! For "they were afraid." That's it. The addendum to Mark's gospel, which doesn't show up in the earliest copies, has Jesus appearing to Mary

Magdalene and two other men, but when these three report in, the disciples don't believe any of them. Finally, Jesus interrupts his men during a meal and chastises them for doubting.

Matthew's account doesn't match either of these. He has two women—one named "the other Mary"—who go to the tomb. There is an earthquake. An angel appears, moves the stone door, and then sits on it. The guards from the temple, who were sent to guard the tomb, see this angel. It terrifies them so much they shake and fall down like dead men. The angel tells the women to send the disciples to Galilee, but as the women go they meet Jesus, who tells them the same thing.

Luke, a Gentile physician and historian who was not one of Jesus' men or, as far as we know, at the crucifixion, is cautious. There are women. They go to the tomb. Jesus isn't there. Angels appear and announce he is "risen." The disciples don't believe these women, except for Peter who runs to the tomb alone, sees it is empty, and then leaves wondering about it all.

It is the most important morning of their lives, but even decades later Jesus' men cannot seem to agree about what happened.

What they do agree about is that it was not their finest hour.

No one believes anyone about anything they say they have seen. The disciples hear that Jesus is alive from people they have known for years, but the next day they are still hiding from the Jews behind locked doors. The women are the only ones showing courage and this is in a culture that doesn't regard them as equal to men. Peter is wracked with guilt and Thomas is filled with doubt and the only thing most of the disciples can think of to do is to go back to their original job: fishing. It is easy to conclude that Jesus could only get his men to pay attention by doing something interesting with food.

It is not much to show for years of teaching and a grisly death. Not yet, anyway. Not in the first days after Jesus died.

But something did happen. Something. We know, in part, because things start to change rapidly and they change among the same band of incompetents who cannot seem to pull it together right after their leader dies.

A regular meeting of Jesus' followers forms right in the temple courts. There was hardly a more dangerous place. The courts were still run by Annas, who had engineered Jesus' death. It took courage to meet there, which the disciples started displaying along with gifts for leading, teaching, and doing miracles.

They got organized. They met each other's needs. They opened their homes and sold property to make it all work. Rich, poor, natives, foreigners, Jews, Gentiles, males, females, slave and free, ex-prostitutes—all formed some kind of living entity. Even their enemies joined them: priests, Samaritans, Syrians, Roman soldiers and, amazingly, the Pharisees.

They never stopped being as human as they were on that memorable Sunday. Sometimes they fought, sometimes they lied, and sometimes they betrayed each other. A few got drunk in meetings and even slept with their father's wives. Others grasped for position. Some were cowards. Yet always they were growing, maturing, urging each other toward the things Jesus had said.

And they were murdered. By the hundreds. And sometimes as hideously as their leader had been. His threat to Israel and Rome lived on through his followers and so they were treated as he had been—with conspiracies and lies and death.

The good that they were, they attributed to the way he died. What they lacked they blamed on not living up to the way he died. His death and resurrection was everything to them. One of their leaders even said it was really all that was important about them: Jesus and the meaning of his death.

The comedian Lenny Bruce once said, "If Jesus had been killed twenty years ago, Catholic schoolchildren would be wearing little electric chairs around their necks instead of crosses." None of this was intended kindly—toward Jesus or Catholics or folks who wear crosses. But he was right.

He said this repeatedly during the late 1950s and early 1960s. So, if Jesus was killed, say, in 1935—beaten with tire irons and stripped of his flesh with farm tools and then electrocuted for 6 hours in public—more than just Catholic schoolchildren would be wearing little images of electric chairs around their necks. But Jesus would still have died and for the same reasons. People who believed in him would still want to commemorate his death.

But he didn't die in 1935. He died in the Jewish year 3790 and the Roman year 784. And a few days after he died, there were two men walking down a road. We know one of them is named Cleopas but we don't know who he is, nor do we know anything about the man with him. There's a hint that both of them are part of a larger group of disciples beyond the twelve.

They are on a walk of about two hours from Jerusalem to the village of Emmaus. And they are deeply disillusioned. Their faces show it and it is all they can talk about. Things did not turn out as they expected.

Then, we are told, a man walks up to them on the road and asks them what they are talking about. The two men don't even try to be friendly.

Are you the only guy in the world who doesn't know what's happening?

The newcomer asks the rude fellow to explain. The two men unload. They are upset about this man Jesus of Nazareth. He was amazing. Did miracles and spoke powerfully. Talked about things to come. Then the chief priests and rulers killed him.

That's all bad enough, they explain, but then just that morning—this is the "third day," Sunday—it started to get weird. Women went to this man's tomb but he wasn't there. They claimed angels appeared to them in a "vision." A few of the men went to the tomb to follow up on what the women said, and they reported it was true. Jesus was gone.

The line that cuts to the heart is this: "We had hoped that he was the one who was going to redeem Israel."

We had hoped.

These two men, and just about everyone else who followed Jesus, is living at this moment on the basis of what he said, despite the horrors they've seen. And some of them just can't hang on anymore. These two men can't, and they're not happy about it. They're confused and disgusted.

We had hoped.

The newcomer isn't too sympathetic. He lets them have it. *Why are you so dull? Didn't Jesus himself say these things had to happen?* Then the stranger starts at the beginning with Moses and goes through all the teachings of the prophets. He explains why Jesus needed to endure everything he did just the way he endured it.

They arrive at Emmaus and the stranger starts to go his way. The two men don't want the conversation to end. Since the day is almost over anyway, they urge the man to stay with them.

He does and they end up eating dinner together. When the stranger takes some bread, thanks God for it, breaks it, and gives them each a piece, they see who it is. It's Jesus. He's back! And then he disappears.

The two are stunned and can't stop talking about how they felt while he was with them. But that's beside the point. He's back!

And it had to happen this way. That's what he said. It was all meant to be, horrible though it was. This idea took the pain away. They weren't living through the most colossal failure of their lives. It all had to be!

They go back to Jerusalem and tell the rest of Jesus' men that it's true. The women were right. Jesus is not dead. And they tell the story of how they saw Jesus "in the breaking of the bread."

Food again.

This is the whole story. Jesus lives for about thirty years, teaches publicly for about two, and then dies a horrid death. His followers keep meeting to honor him but they've got serious problems—like they can't even agree about what happened the day they all say he came back to life. Then they have moral problems. And problems of philosophy. And problems of ego and competition like everyone else.

It is a wonder they ever survived. But they did, because it kept coming back to the same few important matters. No matter how disgusted and disillusioned they were, no matter how far things went from what they were led to expect, Jesus kept showing up. Usually around food, usually teaching something from the scriptures and almost always leaving people changed. And they couldn't deny their experience. He kept showing up. Him. The one who barely had much of a body left when he died. The one they put in the tomb with their own hands. The one whose blood they had to wash off their clothes.

His death was their one great certainty. Then it became the fact that he returned. They never did get their stories straight about that Sunday. And they argued about philosophy and everything else for centuries. They still do, but for most of them there are two certainties: he was dead and then he came back.

Josephus said it well as their movement began:

But those who had become his disciples did not abandon him. They reported that he had appeared to them
three days after his crucifixion and that he was alive.
Accordingly, he was perhaps the Messiah, concerning
whom the prophets wonder. And the tribe of the Christians, so named after him, has not disappeared to this
day.

ANCIENT AUTHORS ON THE DEATH OF JESUS

Though this is not a book of apologetics—a defense of the Bible's historical accuracy and message—it is a book written in the confidence that the crucifixion of Jesus actually occurred. The four gospels provide sufficient evidence of this, but they do not stand alone. Non-Christian writers from near the time of Jesus also mentioned his crucifixion and it is helpful to know what they said. Their words not only give us a window into the Roman world, the world of the Christian Church's birth, but they also remind us how much biblical truth rests upon biblical claims about history.

It is also helpful to have confirmation of the crucifixion of Jesus from writers who were hostile to Christianity. If critics of the faith dismiss those early writers who were sympathetic to Christianity—because they might have distorted facts or been gullible to myth in their eagerness to serve a cause—they cannot dismiss those hostile to Christianity as easily. Enemies of the faith had nothing to gain when they mentioned the crucifixion of Jesus as a historical fact. They were usually stating facts accepted as true in their time and stating these facts by way of prosecuting the early Christians. Their confirmation—that there was a Jesus, that he was crucified under Pontius Pilate, that a movement in Jesus' name arose after his death—is valuable and ought to be regarded as weighty evidence by both Christians and non-Christians alike.

The following, then, are the five earliest and most attested references to the crucifixion of Jesus by non-Christian writers. There are many other early references to Jesus in writings from the period represented below, but these have been chosen because they specifically refer to the crucifixion of Jesus.

1. Josephus – Jewish-Roman Historian

"Now, there was about this time Jesus, a wise man, if it be lawful to call him a man, for he was a doer of wonderful works—a teacher of such men as receive the truth with pleasure. He drew over to him both many of the Jews, and many of the Gentiles. He was [the] Christ and when Pilate, at the suggestion of the principal men amongst us, had condemned him to the cross, those that loved him at the first did not forsake him, for he appeared to them alive again the third day, as the divine prophets had foretold these and ten thousand other wonderful things concerning him; and the tribe of Christians, so named from him, are not extinct at this day."

—*Testimonium Flavianum, Antiquities* 18.3.3 (94 AD)

2. Cornelius Tacitus – Roman Historian

"But not all the relief that could come from man, not all the bounties that the prince could bestow, nor all the atonements which could be presented to the gods, availed to relieve Nero from the infamy of being believed to have ordered the conflagration, the fire of Rome. Therefore, to scotch the rumor, Nero substituted as culprits, and punished with the utmost refinements of cruelty, a class of men, loathed for their vices, whom the crowd styled Christians. Christus, the founder of the name, had undergone the death penalty in the reign of Tiberius, by sentence of the procurator Pontius Pilatus, and the pernicious superstition was checked for a moment, only to break out once more, not merely in Judaea, the home of the disease, but in the capital itself, where all things horrible or shameful in the world collect and find a vogue."

—*Annals* 15.44, Loeb Edition (116 AD)

3. Lucian of Samasota – Satirist

"The Christians, you know, worship a man to this day— the distinguished personage who introduced their novel rites, and was crucified on that account . . . You see, these misguided creatures . . . worship the crucified sage, and live after his laws."

—*The Death of Peregrine*, 11–13 (170 AD)

4. Mara Bar-Serapion – Philosopher

"What advantage did the Athenians gain from putting Socrates to death? Famine and plague came upon them as a judgment for their crime. What advantage did the men of Samos gain from burning Pythagoras? In a moment their land was covered with sand. What advantage did the Jews gain from executing their wise King?

It was just after that that their kingdom was abolished. God justly avenged these three wise men: the Athenians died of hunger; the Samians were overwhelmed by the sea; the Jews, ruined and driven from their land, live in complete dispersion. But Socrates did not die for good; he lived on in the teaching of Plato. Pythagoras did not die for good; he lived on in the statue of Hera. Nor did the wise King die for good; He lived on in the teaching which He had given."

–British Museum Syriac MS. Addition 14,658

(just after 70 AD)

5. The Talmud

"It has been taught: On the eve of Passover they hanged Yeshu. And an announcer went out, in front of him, for forty days (saying): 'He is going to be stoned, because he practiced sorcery and enticed and led Israel astray. Anyone who knows anything in his favor, let him come and plead in his behalf.' But, not having found anything in his favor, they hanged him on the eve of Passover.

–Babylonian Talmud: Sanhedrin 43a (70–200 AD)

NOTES

Complete information about publications mentioned in the Notes can be found in the Bibliography beginning on page 247.

Prologue

1   ***Just as the empire intended:*** "Whenever we crucify the condemned, the most crowded roads are chosen, where the most people can see and be moved by this terror. For penalties relate not so much to retribution as to their exemplary effect." (Ps. Quintilian, *Declamations* 274; Ps. Manetho, Apotelesmatica 4.198–200; Aristophanes, *Thesmophoriazusae* 1029, quoted in Craig A. Evans, "Crucifixion," in Katherine Doob Sakenfeld, ed., *The New Interpreter's Dictionary of the Bible*, 1:807.)

Chronology of a Conspiracy

9   ***John, later known as "the Baptist":*** One of the great oddities of our western calendars is that the birth of Christ comes years "before Christ." We can thank Dionysius Exiguus for this. He was the Roman abbot who in 527 AD made the computations that produced the Julian calendar—in which Jesus was born four years before Christ! Dionysius can be forgiven. His sources were flawed. Every scholar knows the feeling. Also, the corrected calendar aligned more closely with the dates reported in Scripture. So, all is well.

10   *charging Jesus with blasphemy:* Luke 5:21.

10   *Jesus heals a man on the Sabbath:* Mark 3:1–6.

10   *accuse Jesus of being demon possessed:* Mark 3:22.

10   *Jesus declares publicly that there is a conspiracy:* John 7:19–20, John 8:36–37, 40.

10   *He ministers mainly in Galilee to avoid capture:* John 7:1.

10   *Pharisees warn Jesus:* Luke 13:31–33.

10   *He escapes and leaves Jerusalem:* John 10:31, 39–40.

11   *a meeting at the house of Caiaphas:* Matthew 26:3–5.

11   *9th of Nisan:* "Nisan" is a thirty-day month in the Hebrew calendar. Nisan, the month in which Passover occurs, is a spring month, falling during March and April on the Gregorian calendar.

11   *chief priests and scribes search for opportunity:* Mark 14:1–2.

11   *13th of Nisan:* The Hebrew day begins at sunset, as it did at Jesus' time. This means that while his men prepared for the Passover meal on one day, it was the next day—and date—when they ate it after sundown.

CHAPTER 1

Inceptum: **The Beginning**

13   *March, 750 Years Since the Founding of Rome (A.U.C.):* The Romans understood history as originating with the founding of the city of Rome. Their dates were computed, then, "from the founding of the city"—*ab urbe conditae*, or "AUC." The year 750 AUC is 3758 in the Hebrew calendar and 4 BC in the Gregorian calendar.

13   *slow fire that actually emits a glow:* This entire description of

Herod the Great's maladies comes from Josephus, *Antiquities* 17.168. The reference to a fire inside of Herod is odd. It would appear that Josephus is describing a fever were it not for the reference to a "glow." His exact words are, "for a fire glowed in him slowly, which did not so much appear to the touch outwardly, as it augmented his pains inwardly."

16   ***cause sorrow and pain:*** Herod died before this order was carried out. His children sent his intended victims home in peace.

16   ***safer to be Herod's pig:*** Josephus wrote that when Herod heard of Antipater's betrayal, "he cried out, and beat his head, although he was at death's door, and raised himself upon his elbow, and sent for some of his guards, and commanded them to kill Antipater without any further delay, and to do it presently, and to bury him in an ignoble manner at Hyrcania" (*Antiquities* 17.187). The comment by Augustus is not only a pun in the original Greek but also an insult aimed at Herod's Jewishness. As a Jew, Herod was not permitted to own a pig. Augustus knew this and insinuated that Herod owned one anyway.

19   ***weeping for her dismembered sons:*** Matthew 2:18, a quote from Jeremiah 31:15—"A voice is heard in Ramah, weeping and great mourning, Rachel weeping for her children and refusing to be comforted, because they are no more." For more on this "Slaughter of the Innocents," see Paul L. Maier, "Herod and the Infants of Bethlehem", in *Chronos, Kairos, Christos II.*

19   ***believing he has killed his rival:*** Herod died in March of 750 AUC, or 4 BC. The eastern magician-priests, the "Magi," must have first seen their star, then, in 748 AUC. For a fascinating discussion of this star by a professor of astronomy at the University of Minnesota, see the late Karlis Kaufmanis' article "The Star of Bethlehem," which appeared in *Christmas: An American Annual of Literature and*

Art (vol. 43, 1973, Augsburg Publishing House) and was reprinted in the *Minnesota Astronomy Review* (Vol. 18, 2003/2004), a publication of the Department of Astronomy at the University of Minnesota.

CHAPTER 2

Piaculum: **The Sacrifice**

21   ***tax man who caused the big delay:*** The Mishnah, the "oral Torah" or the transcribed oral traditions of rabbinic Judaism, insists that "if a tax-gatherer enters a house, the house becomes unclean." This is indicative of how most Jews viewed the publicans—Jews who profited by collecting exorbitant taxes from their own people. That "the one the authorities seek" would have a publican among his men and spend a night in a publican's house was radical. It is important to remember that his behavior challenged only the oral tradition of the rabbis and not the revealed law of God. From Tohoroth 7.6, in H. Danby, *The Mishnah*, 726.

22   ***changed everything in Zakkai's life:*** The name "Zakkai" is used here not only to introduce us to the name Jesus likely used for the man but also to help us see this story and stories like it afresh. Tales we have heard all our lives, Bible stories in particular, can wear ruts into our minds. We stop hearing them—we stop allowing the words to paint their pictures—and instead we let them pass by nearly unnoticed. "Blind Bartimaeus," for example, was actually named Bar Timaeus. It is a small change but it is accurate to the original and it reminds us that he was named after his father, a man we would call "Timothy" in today's English. This man's son was born blind and ended up a beggar. The name Bar Timaeus evokes more of the intended drama by focusing our attention on the father. The same is true of Zakkai. It means "the just," yet Zakkai was a man who charged his fellow Jews inflated Roman taxes to make outlandish profits for himself. "The just"? We can see the irony, just as scripture intended. This is the benefit of using original names, which we will do wherever possible in this text.

23   ***They decided to kill Lazarus:*** John 12:10.

24   ***pure nard—and shockingly expensive:*** The single bottle of nard poured on the rabbi at Bethany was three hundred times the average daily wage of the time. This is what prompted the comment, probably by Judas, that the nard "could have been sold for more than a year's wages and the money given to the poor" (Mark 14:5).

25   ***he allowed this to happen once before:*** Luke 7:36–38.

CHAPTER 3

Illegitimus: **The Illegitimate**

28   ***the Greeks called him* Iesous:** The Romans also referred to Jesus as "Christus."

28   ***some call him Mary's Bastard:*** The charge that Jesus was a bastard circulated during his lifetime and long after. In *The Babylonian Talmud*, which was compiled from 70 AD to approximately 200 AD, a Rabbi Shimeon Ben Azzai wrote of Jesus Christ: "I found a genealogical roll in Jerusalem wherein was recorded, Such-an-one is a bastard of an adulteress" (b.Yebamoth 49a; m Yebam. 4:13). Another passage insists that Mary, the mother of Jesus, who was "the descendant of princes and governors, played the harlot with carpenters" (b. Sanh. 106a). Also: "His mother was Miriam, a women's hairdresser. As they say, . . . 'this one strayed from her husband'" (b. Sabb. 104b).

32   ***he was "the carpenter's son":*** Matthew 13:53–57.

33   ***they thought he was losing his mind:*** Mark 3:20–21.

CHAPTER 4

Urbs: **The City**

37   ***home to some twenty-five thousand:*** Joachim Jeremias, *Jerusalem in the Time of Jesus*, 27.

38   ***built an opulent palace for himself:*** It was so impressive that the Roman governor chose to live there whenever he was in Jerusalem rather than in the suites maintained for him at the Fortress of Antonia. His name was Pontius Pilate.

38   ***the daunting Fortress of Antonia:*** The Fortress of Antonia had watchtowers that were more than a hundred feet high and included apartments, shops, barracks, armories, and a cistern that collected rain forty feet below street level.

38   ***Ten thousand men work on her:*** Josephus, *Antiquities* 15.390; The Temple of Jerusalem took more than a century to build and was not finished until 64 AD. When the work was done, more than eighteen thousand men were laid off. The economic impact upon the region was devastating.

38   ***often called "a city of palaces":*** The ugly gash upon Jerusalem was its Lower City. There on the city's south side, the poor and the disregarded lived. It was a slum, a warren of narrow alleys, meager dwellings, and blighted lives. There were shops, fruit stands, workshops, and even synagogues. But the stench told the story. The Lower City notoriously smelled of feces and blood. Criminal gangs roamed. Outlaw chiefs ruled territory with venom. The Lower City seemed worlds away from the elite, elegant Upper City to the west and the sanctified realms of the temple to the northeast.

38   ***the markets and the ornate baths:*** By the time of Jesus, Jerusalem had become a thriving center of trade. This was also a gift of the Herods, who were quick to notice that during feast seasons the city

might grow to seven times its usual population. It took no special gift to see that the same roads that brought religious pilgrims from every nation could also bring merchants. With plans for a global trade center in mind, the Herods enlisted the merchants of Jerusalem. Soon foreign markets opened to Israel's wheat, honey, dried fruits, olive oil, and balsam. In return came beer from Medea and Egypt, garments from India, wood and apples from Crete, and similar goods from dozens of other lands. The City of David became a city of trade respected throughout the civilized world.

39   ***all the people of Israel:*** At this time, the average man was five feet four inches tall and weighed 135 pounds. The average woman was five feet tall and weighed less than a hundred pounds. Even their lifespans were short. The average age was twenty-eight. If a child lived past age fifteen, he was likely to live to the age of fifty-six. Less than half did.

39   ***as many as fifty million:*** John Reader, *Cities*, 83.

39   ***Jews account for only 6 to 12 percent:*** Louis H. Feldman, *Jew and Gentile in the Ancient World*, 293.

40   ***sometimes backward minority:*** The truth is that the Jews of the first century were far ahead of Rome in a variety of important fields. Medicine was a shining example. The typical Roman was comparatively primitive in his view of science, suspecting a physician as he might a palm reader. He preferred home remedies and had no more regard for a man of science than he had for a magician. By contrast, the Sanhedrin required every village to support a doctor. This led to an eagerness to learn from medical advances in other parts of the world. Surgeons throughout the Mediterranean lands had already learned to amputate limbs and seal off arteries. Doctors routinely used anesthetics like nepenthe and mandragora. With new procedures came new instruments. Surgeons used needles for suturing,

forceps for delivering babies, catheters, surgical scissors, and ratchets for dilation. In Egypt, surgeons were successfully performing operations on the human brain as well as tracheotomies. Hebrew doctors mastered these techniques and returned innovations of their own. They were among the first to operate on the human eye for cataracts. They had used false teeth half a millennium before but made improvements by using teeth from animals and the dead. Far ahead of their time, they urged dental hygiene and the use of a honey-based toothpaste. The people of Israel proved themselves brilliant innovators in a number of fields. By the time of Jesus, they had mastered the use of concrete, a Roman invention of two centuries earlier. They employed waterpower with such finesse that their machines crushed olives without breaking the pits and ruining the oil. They became experts in the use of the Roman *machine tractoria*, the crane, and dared to make improvements of their own. They even modified standard designs for harnesses and saddles to enable horses to run faster and live longer.

CHAPTER 5

Imperium: **The Empire**

44 ***Pontius Pilate, the Prefect of Judea:*** There has occasionally been question as to whether Pontius Pilate actually existed. Is there evidence for him apart from the Bible? Yes. He is mentioned in Josephus: "Now there was about this time Jesus, a wise man . . . And when Pilate, at the suggestion of the principal men amongst us, had condemned him to the cross, those that loved him at the first did not forsake him . . ." (*Antiquities* 18.63). He is also mentioned in the writings of the Roman historian Tacitus: "Christus, the founder of the [Christian] name, was put to death by Pontius Pilate, procurator of Judea in the reign of Tiberius" (*Annals* XV. 44). The Jewish philosopher Philo refers to Pilate's "inflexible, stubborn and cruel disposition" and to the fact that he was known for "venality, thefts, assaults, abusive behavior and his frequent murders of untried prisoners" (*Legacy to Gaius* 38.302). There is also archaeological evidence: a stone bearing an inscription attributed to Pilate was found in 1961 in Caesarea. The stone was part of a temple that Pilate built for the Roman Emperor Tiberius. Though the inscription is worn in places, scholars have determined that it reads: "To the honorable gods this Tiberium Pontius Pilate, Prefect of Judea, had dedicated" (See Craig A. Evans, *Jesus and the Ossuaries*, 45–47).

44   ***multitudes of Jews rushed to Caesarea:*** Josephus, *Antiquities* 18.55–59.

45   ***aqueduct to be paid for out of temple funds:*** The issue for the Jews was that temple funds were considered *corban*, dedicated to God. For Pilate to presumptuously use these funds to build an aqueduct was a blasphemous offense.

45   ***thousands of Jews gathered to protest:*** Josephus, *Antiquities* 18.60–62.

46   ***last appointment Valerius Gratas made:*** *Antiquities* 18.34–35. "This man deprived Ananus of the high priesthood, and appointed Ismael, the son of Phabi, to be high priest. He also deprived him in a little time, and ordained Eleazar, the son of Ananus, who had been high priest before, to be high priest: which office, when he had held for a year, Gratus deprived him of it, and gave the high priesthood to Simon, the son of Camithus; and when he had possessed that dignity no longer than a year, Joseph Caiaphas was made his successor. When Gratus had done those things, he went back to Rome, after he had tarried in Judea eleven years, when Pontius Pilate came as his successor." Among the more interesting archaeological finds relating to biblical figures was the November 1990 discovery of a crypt

containing twelve ossuaries (bone boxes) in Jerusalem's Peace Forest. The inscriptions include "Joseph son of Cayafa" and "Joseph son of Qafa." The majority opinion among scholars seems to be that these ossuaries relate to the family of Caiaphas, son-in-law of Annas. For further discussion of this discovery and its implications, see Craig A. Evans, *Jesus and His World: The Archaeological Evidence*, 97.

48   *great march from Caesarea each year:* In this narrative of the two processions into Jerusalem, I'm grateful for the groundbreaking work of Marcus Borg and John Dominic Crossan in their *The Last Week: The Day-By-Day Account of Jesus's Final Week in Jerusalem*.

48   *when 8,500 men were killed:* E. P. Sanders, *The Historical Figure of Jesus*, 23–26.

49   *the Praetorium—Herod's Palace:* The exact location of the Jerusalem Praetorium in the day of Jesus has long been a matter of debate. In Caesarea, the Praetorium was unquestionably Herod's Palace, where the apostle Paul was later held prisoner. Scholars largely agree about this. In Jerusalem, though, both the Fortress Antonia and Herod's magnificent palace in the Upper City are candidates and scholars tend to be divided on the matter.

The Fortress has the support of tradition, particularly the medieval invention of the Via Dolorosa. Antonia as the Praetorium also makes stories about Jesus—his trials and crucifixion, for example—far easier to track geographically since it was mere inches from the temple and on the side of Jerusalem closest to the Mount of Olives.

However, the case is stronger for Herod's Palace as Jerusalem's Praetorium. It was the finest private home in the city, which is why Rome appropriated it along with other palaces in Jerusalem. Josephus tells us that the Roman Prefects lived in Herod's Palace and judged cases from a seat on the elevated pavement in front of the house (Josephus, *Wars* 2.301). And there seems to be greater biblical support for Herod's Palace. Consider Mark 15:16 for example: "The soldiers led Jesus away into the palace (that is, the Praetorium) and called together the whole company of soldiers."

Some scholars have suggested that the building designated as the Praetorium changed with each visit of the Roman Prefect. If this is true, we should remember that Pilate's wife was with him on the visit to Jerusalem during which he ruled in the matter of Jesus Christ. He surely would have chosen the opulence of Herod's Palace over the far less refined Fortress Antonia, if only to please her. She was Caesar Augustus' granddaughter and used to the finer things. Pilate would have wanted the most comfortable option for her. This would have meant Herod's Palace.

CHAPTER 6

Regnum: **The Kingdom**

53   *image of King Solomon riding:* 1 Kings 1:33–44.

53   *Rejoice greatly, Daughter Zion!:* Zechariah 9:9.

54   *Hosanna! Blessed is he who comes:* Mark 11:9b–10.

55   *particularly thrilling Passover procession:* Josephus, *Antiquities* 17.213–217.

57   *a carefully crafted demonstration:* Alfred Edersheim, a nineteenth-century Jewish convert to Christianity who became an Anglican priest and scholar, wrote of this in the language of the Victorian era: "From the moment of His sending forth the two disciples to His acceptance of the homage of the multitude, and His rebuke of the Pharisee's attempt to arrest it, all must be regarded as designed or approved by Him: not only a public assertion of His Messiahship, but a claim to its national acknowledgement" (*Life and Times of Jesus*, 729).

CHAPTER 7

Pontifex: **The Priest**

60   *and the tributes owed to Rome:* "And, beginning in 6 CE, the temple and temple authorities were also the center of the imperial tax system. They had the responsibility for collecting and paying the annual tribute due to Rome." (Borg, Marcus J.; Crossan, John Dominic. *The Last Week: What the Gospels Really Teach About Jesus's Final Days in Jerusalem.* New York: HarperOne, 2007.)

62   *high priesthood of Annas and Caiaphas:* Luke 3:2; Acts 4:6.

62   *riding into the Holy City:* Mark 11:1–10 (NRSV).

62   *twisting Isaiah's song of the vineyard:* Mark 12:1–12; Isaiah 5:1–7.

63   *sent the Pharisees over the edge:* The Herodians were wealthy, influential Jews who benefited from Herod's reign and identified publicly with it. To them, Jesus was both a political threat and bad for business. The Pharisees were "separated ones," as their name indicates in Aramaic. They were fanatical about observing every requirement of the law and yet not only did so with sinful pride but also thought nothing of adding requirements of their own to the law of God. They believed in divine foreordination, in the immortality of the soul, in the resurrection of the body, and in supernatural beings. They angered Jesus more than the Herodians—who were moved by influence and wealth—and the Sadducees—the religious rationalists of their age—because these Pharisees were closer to the will of God but kept from salvation by their pride and unloving hearts.

64   *Bazaars of the Family of Annas:* Alfred Edersheim has written, "there can be little doubt, that this market was what in Rabbinic writings is styled 'the Bazaars of the sons of Annas' (*Chanuyoth beney Chanan*), the sons of that high-priest Annas, who is so infamous in New Testament history. When we read that the Sanhedrin, forty years before the destruction of Jerusalem, transferred its meeting-place from 'the Hall of Hewn Stones' (on the south side of the Court of the Priest, and therefore partly within the Sanctuary itself) to 'the Bazaars,' and then afterwards to the City, the inference is plain that these Bazaars were those of the sons of Annas the high-priest, and that they occupied part of the Temple-court; in short, that the Temple-market and the Bazaars of the sons of Annas are identical" (Edersheim, *Life and Times of Jesus*, 257).

65   ***the Empire of Annas:*** "He was a great hoarder up of money . . . he also had servants who were very wicked, who joined themselves to the boldest sort of the people, and went to the thrashing-floors, and took away the tithes that belonged to the priests by violence, and did not refrain from beating such as would not give these tithes to them. So the other high priests acted in the like manner, as did those his servants, without any one being able to prohibit them; so that [some of the] priests, that of old were wont to be supported with those tithes, died for want of food" (Josephus, *Antiquities* 20.2040).

CHAPTER 8

Advenae: **The Foreigners**

69   ***the scribes, and even the Essenes:*** The Essenes have been described as "the monks of Israel." Their name means "holy ones" in Aramaic original. At the time of Jesus, they numbered about four thousand, lived in the wilderness, and usually did not marry. They built communities in remote places where they sustained themselves by the work of their own hands.

They wanted above all to keep from the defilement of the world and to live according to God's law. Their habits were simple, their food and clothing plain, and they lived so as to regulate every moment of the day for God. The scribes were, as their name suggests, people who could write. This was a valuable skill at a time when most people were illiterate.

Scribes sometimes set up tables by the side of the road to offer services like writing letters and copying legal documents. They also copied the scriptures and rabbinic works to keep these valuable legacies from being lost through decay and destruction. This meant that they knew law and history well. In fact, in the New Testament, they are called "experts in the law," and, eventually "lawyers" (Luke 7:30).

71 *only courtyard open to Gentiles:* Josephus, *Apion* 2.104–106.

71 *Foreigners must not enter:* Evans, *Jesus and His World*, 91.

72 *the Tyrian silver shekel:* The Tyrian shekel was the coin of choice in the temple because it had more silver in it than any other. A silver coin from Antioch, for example, was somewhere around 80 percent silver, and loose standards allowed this to vary from coin to coin. The Tyrian shekel was 90 percent silver and its production was tightly controlled to make sure each coin was exactly the same (Richardson, *Building Jewish in the Roman East*, 247).

72 *Tyre hates all Jews:* Josephus, *Wars* 4.105.

73 *a "den of robbers":* Jeremiah 7:11.

74 *house of prayer for all nations:* Isaiah 56:3–7.

CHAPTER 9

Coniuratus: **The Conspiracy**

81 *he did nothing:* Mark 11:11.

CHAPTER 10

Occursus: **The Meeting**

85 *nine years he was high priest:* Annas served as high priest from 6 AD to 15 AD, when the Romans replaced him.

87 *choice positions of power:* Joachim Jeremias, *Jerusalem in the Time of Jesus*, 98.

87 *Pharisees tried to kill the Galilean:* Matthew 12:14.

88 *the Herodians joined them:* Mark 3:5–6.

88 *a wonder anyone follows them:* Josephus wrote about this, "What I would now explain is this, that the Pharisees have delivered to the people a great many observances by succession from their fathers, which are not written in the law of Moses; and for that reason it is that the Sadducees reject them and say that we are to esteem those observances to be obligatory which are in the written word, but are not to observe what are derived from the tradition of our forefathers; and concerning these things it is that great disputes and differences have arisen among them, while the Sadducees are able to persuade none but the rich, and have not the populace obsequious to them, but the Pharisees have the multitude on their side . . ." (*Antiquities* 13.297– 298).

89 *To be a Sadducee requires intelligence:* Josephus said that the Sadducees were "received but by a few, yet by those still of the greatest dignity" (Josephus, *Antiquities* 18.16–17).

89 *best that things remain as they are:* When the Sadducees were forced into positions of authority in the more rural areas, they often started to behave like Pharisees. It was so difficult to maintain their more rationalist theology and upper-crust ways that they surrendered for convenience and took on the ways of the opposition. Josephus recounts, "When they become magistrates, as they are unwillingly and by force sometimes obliged to be, they addict themselves to the notions of the Pharisees, because the multitude would not otherwise bear them" (Josephus, *Antiquities* 18.17).

89   ***doesn't believe that the future is determined:*** "And for the Sadducees, they take away fate, and say there is no such thing, and that the events of human affairs are not at its disposal; but they suppose that all our actions are in our own power, so that we are ourselves the cause of what is good, and receive what is evil from our own folly" (Josephus, *Antiquities* 13.173).

90   ***Sadducees know such things do not occur:*** "The doctrine of the Sadducees is this," wrote Josephus: "that souls die with the bodies" (*Antiquities* 18.16).

90   ***typical Sadducee rudeness:*** Josephus reported that the Sadducees "in their intercourse with their peers are as rude as to aliens."

91   ***Caiaphas is incensed:*** There is a portion of Josephus—one of our few sources on the Sadducees—that gives us insight into the character of the Hanan Dynasty. This is the family of corrupt high priests begun by Annas. "Now the report goes, that this elder Annas proved a most fortunate man; for he had five sons, who had all performed the office of a high priest to God, and he had himself enjoyed that dignity a long time formerly, which had never happened to any other of our high priests: but this younger Annas, who, as we have told you already took the high priesthood, was a bold man in his temper, and very insolent; he was also of the sect of the Sadducees, who are very rigid in judging offenders, above all the rest of the Jews, as we have already observed" (*Antiquities* 20.198–199). The "elder Annas" is Annas the father-in-law of Caiaphas. The "younger Annas" is his son, who served as high priest years later. He continued his father's traditions, though. He was the man who executed James, the brother of Jesus.

92   *a "man of Kerioth":* Edersheim, *Life and Times of Jesus*, 361.

93   *teaching such odd things:* John 6:53–66.

93   *allowed women to travel with him:* Luke 8:1–3.

94   *What are you willing to give me:* Matthew 26:14–15.

94   *rate for the purchase of a slave:* Edersheim, *Life and Times of Jesus*, 803. See also Zechariah 11:12. This price was set in Exodus 21:32.

CHAPTER 11

Oraculum: The Teachings

95   *when he was a child:* Luke 2:46.

96   *forced out the merchants:* John 2:13–22.

96   *at a well talking to a woman:* John 4:1–26.

96   *he had to be "born again":* John 3:1–21.

96   *healed a lame man on the Sabbath:* John 5:1–14.

97   *he decided to pick grain:* Matthew 12:1–8.

97   *healed a man's hand:* Matthew 12:9–14.

97   *Roman officers came to him:* Luke 7:1–10.

97   *widow's son back from the dead:* Luke 7:11–17.

97   *woman with a colorful past:* Luke 7:36–50.

97   *His mother and brothers went:* Mark 3:31–35.

98   *told a story about dirt:* Mark 4:1–20.

98   *the righteous shouldn't pay taxes:* Matthew 22:17–22.

98   *tried to make him king by force:* John 6:15

98   *her sins were forgiven:* John 8:2–11.

98   *blindness wasn't caused by sin:* John 9:2–7.

99   *couldn't stop using the word "bastard":* John 8:41.

99   *accused him of having a demon:* Luke 3:22; John 8:48; John 10:20.

100   *called them blind guides:* Matthew 15:14.

100   *compared them to serpents:* Matthew 23:33.

100   *urged the people to simply ignore them:* Matthew 16:11.

100   *kingdom was going to be taken:* Matthew 21:43.

101   *longed to gather your children:* Luke 13:34.

CHAPTER 12

Proditio: The Betrayal

104   *much shame on this night:* The "young man" running away from soldiers in Mark 14:51 is likely the apostle Mark himself. It is not stated plainly in scripture and therefore is not certain. Still, it is likely. It is also pleasant to think that the odd mention of a naked man in an otherwise tragic tale is the personal reflection of an older man remembering the most harrowing moment of his life. If this is true, then we should hold this episode up against the other mentions of Mark in the New Testament: that he was the son of a wealthy family well known in the early church (Acts 12:12); that he was the cousin of Barnabas (Colossians 4:10); that he accompanied Paul and Barnabas on their first missionary journey but then abandoned them (Acts 13:13); that he was at the heart of the breach between Paul and Barnabas (Acts 15:36); that he went with Barnabas to Cyprus (Acts 15:36); that years later Paul worked to restore Mark to the churches (Colossians 4:10); that Mark then worked at Peter's side (1 Peter 5:13); and that Paul said, at the end of his life, that Mark had become "helpful to me in my ministry" (2 Timothy 4:11).

104 ***owner offered it as a haven:*** We envision the Garden of Geth-
semane as something like a public park. Historians of ancient Israel
have long pointed out, though, that an olive press was too valuable a
thing in that day to leave exposed. It must have been privately owned
and walled, with access tightly controlled to protect both the press
itself and the yield of the vegetation. This seems reasonable. Yeshua
very likely knew the press's owner and enjoyed the use of it whenever
he wished. This is not hard to imagine. He had a similar welcome
from the owner of the "upper room" and the owner of a house in
Bethany.

107 ***kissed him, not once but over and over again:*** The word used
is *katephilesen.* Edersheim gives its meaning as "repeatedly, loudly,
effusively."

CHAPTER 13

Vendicta: **The Vengeance**

115 ***There are laws:*** Deuteronomy 19:15: "One witness is not enough
to convict anyone accused of any crime or offense they may have
committed. A matter must be established by the testimony of two or
three witnesses."

115 ***I have spoken openly:*** John 18:20–21.

116 ***bring out your case:*** "One curious feature of legal procedure in the
Sanhedrin was that the man involved was held to be absolutely innocent, and indeed, not even on trial, until the evidence of the witnesses
had been stated and confirmed. The argument about the case could
only begin when the testimony of the witnesses was given and confirmed. That is the point of the conversation between Jesus and Annas
in John 18:19–21. Jesus in that incident was reminding Annas that he
had no right to ask him anything until the evidence of witnesses had

been taken and found to agree." William Barclay, *The Gospel of John* (Edinburgh, 1956), quoted in Leon Morris, *Gospel According to John*, 755.

119 ***nothing about this gathering that is just:*** Two brief examples of legal requirements of the later Sanhedrin help us understand how much its members strained to apply the justice of the law to their proceedings. We cannot be sure that these exact principles governed Sanhedrin rulings in the first century. It is likely, though, that the jurisprudence was similar to this, since both are based upon the same principles from the Torah.

> "After what fashion do they conduct the trial? The judges remain seated with the contending parties standing before them; and the one who brings the charge states his case first. When there are witnesses, these are brought in and admonished. All of them except the chief witness are then sent out, and the judges hear what he has to say and then dismiss him. Afterwards they bring in the two contending parties who state their case in each other's presence. If all the judges decide that the accused is innocent, he is adjudged innocent; and if all the judges decide that he is guilty, he is adjudged guilty. The same applies to non-capital and capital cases.

> "Witnesses cannot be adjudged perjurers until the trial has been completed. They cannot be scourged, fined, or put to death, until the trial has been completed. One of the witnesses cannot be adjudged a perjurer without the other; and one cannot be scourged without the other, or put to death without the other, or fined without the other."

119 ***the House of Hanan:*** Since Annas' Hebrew name was "Hananiah," his family dynasty was known as "The House of Han," a shortened version of his name.

120 *you will see the Son of Man:* Mark 14:62.

Judicium: **The Judgment**

125 *found this man subverting our nation:* Luke 23:2.

129 *uncertain as to who the man is:* Luke 9:7–9.

Excoriare: **The Torture**

133 *already declared the man innocent:* John 19:1–6.

134 *halfway death:* Bishop, *The Day Christ Died*, 277.

136 *Law forbids more than forty lashes:* Deuteronomy 25:2–3: "If the guilty person deserves to be beaten, the judge shall make them lie down and have them flogged in his presence with the number of lashes the crime deserves, but the judge must not impose more than forty lashes. If the guilty party is flogged more than that, your fellow Israelite will be degraded in your eyes."

136 *floggings should be stopped only when:* Tal Ilan, *Jewish Women in Greco-Roman Palestine* (Tübingen, Germany: J. C. B. Mohr, 1995), quoted in Nick Page, *The Longest Week*.

137 *racist slaughter visited on one man:* See Pollard, *Soldiers, Cities, and Civilians*, 120.

137 *bones in Jesus' back are exposed:* It is hard for us to imagine a man scourged so thoroughly that his bones are visible. Still, this is what commonly occurred during the Roman scourging. Josephus tells us of a man, for example, named Jesus ben Ananias who went about prophesying Jerusalem's doom and was eventually taken before the

Roman governor. The man was "whipped till his bones were laid bare" (Josephus, *Wars* 6.304).

140 **prisoner to return to Gabbatha:** *Gabbatha* is Aramaic for "the rounded height" and is used to describe the elevated pavement stone upon which the Roman governors sat to mete out punishment.

CHAPTER 16

Crucio: **The Crucifixion**

144 **Pilate: "Behold, the man":** In Latin, *ecco homo*. In Greek, Ἰδοὺ ὁ ἄνθρωπος (*Idou ho anthrōpos*).

148 **cutting the skin in grief is forbidden:** Leviticus 19:28.

148 **crucified more than eight hundred:** Josephus, *Wars* 1.96.

149 **You must not defile the land:** Deuteronomy 21:22–23 (NRSV).

149 **never rule upon a single sentence of death:** Sanhedrin, VI.4.

150 **Thousands were crucified at his command:** Curtius Rufus, *History of Alexander* 4.4.17.

152 **put the cross upon the slave:** Juvenal, *Satyr* 6. v. 248.

153 **even through his tongue:** Seneca, *Dialogue* 6.

CHAPTER 17

Lamenta: **The Weeping**

156 **guilt of shedding innocent blood:** Deuteronomy 21:9.

157 **Jesus of Nazareth, King of the Jews:** The initials used in Christian liturgy and art as a symbol for Jesus Christ—INRI—come from the first letters of the words on this titulus: *Iesus Nazarenus Rex Iudaeorum*.

158 *word that means "place of the skull":* The word *Calvary* entered Christian vocabulary centuries after Jesus lived. It is taken from the Latin word *Calvariae*, which has the same meaning as Golgotha: "the place of, or the image of, a skull." It entered widespread Christian usage through the King James Bible, which in turn borrowed this Latinized version of *Golgotha* from the Latin Vulgate.

159 *conscript's name is Simon:* Some have suggested that a man of black skin carried the cross for Jesus. We cannot assume this. There were many colonies of light-skinned people in Cyrene. His name, Simon, makes us think he might have been Jewish but we are also told that his sons were Rufus and Alexander and these are pagan names. Jews bore such names, as well. Scholars have debated for years what ethnicity Simon might have been and what he might have been doing in Cyrene. We cannot know with certainty.

160 *Daughters of Jerusalem, do not weep:* Luke 23:28–31.

160 *he repeats the dire prophecy:* It is impossible to explain the great grief Jesus felt over Jerusalem—grief he displayed while entering the city on Palm Sunday and leaving the city for Golgotha less than a week later—without understanding the astonishing devastation that brought her to an end in 70 AD. This occurred just forty years after Jesus was killed. He had warned of it and wept over it constantly. He told Israel's corrupt religious leaders they would be punished by it and he told the early Church how to escape it once it began. Its horrors filled his final thoughts, though he was suffering great horrors of his own at the time.

The classic description of the fall of Jerusalem is Josephus' *The Jewish Wars*. Josephus was an eyewitness to and a participant in that great conflagration. Though even a brief summary of Josephus' writings is beyond the scope of this book, the few quotes below hint at why Jesus was so often overwhelmed by what lay just ahead for his people. These passages describe shocking moments during the three-and-a-half-year Roman siege that ultimately led to the city's fall in 70 AD.

- **The beginning of famine during the siege:** "Famine now raged in the city, and the rebels took all the food they could find in a house-to-house search, while the poor starved to death by the thousands. People gave all their wealth for a little measure of wheat, and hid to eat it hastily and in secret so it would not be taken from them. Wives would snatch the food from their husbands, children from fathers, and mothers from the very mouths of infants."

- **Those who ventured out of the besieged city to find food:** Titus' "troops captured many who ventured out to look for food. When caught, they resisted, and were then tortured and crucified before the walls as a terrible warning to the people within . . . some 500 were captured daily. . . . Out of rage and hatred, the soldiers nailed their prisoners in different postures, and so great was their number that space could not be found for the crosses."

- **Indications of the numbers killed:** "One refugee, who had been in charge of a single gate, told Titus that 115,880 corpses had been carried out in an eleven-week period. Other leaders reported that 600,000 bodies of the lower classes had been thrown out, and it was impossible to number the rest."

- **The extent of starvation:** "A measure of wheat now sold for a talent, and when it was no longer possible to gather herbs after the city was walled in, some searched the sewers for offal or ate old cow dung."

- **The horrors of starvation:** "Maddened by hunger, she

[Mary] seized the infant at her breast and said, 'Poor baby, why should I preserve you for war, famine, and rebellion? Come, be my food—vengeance against the rebels, and the climax of Jewish tragedy for the world.' With that, she killed her infant son, roasted his body, and devoured half of it, hiding the rest."

- **The destruction of the temple:** "While the Temple was in flames, the victors stole everything they could lay their hands on, and slaughtered all who were caught. No pity was shown to age or rank, old men or children, the laity or priests—all were massacred. As the flames roared up, and since the temple stood on a hill, it seemed as if the whole city were ablaze . . . the ground was hidden by corpses, and the soldiers had to climb over heaps of bodies in pursuit of the fugitives."

- **Titus' epitaph over the fall of Jerusalem:** "As Titus entered the city he was astonished at its strength, and especially the towers which the tyrants had abandoned. Indeed, when he saw how high and massive they were, and the size of each huge block, he exclaimed, 'Surely God was with us in the war, who brought the Jews down from these strongholds, for what could hand or engine do against these towers.'"

Josephus' works are widely available in inexpensive editions. His complete works are available for e-readers at no cost at all on most of the major bookseller websites. Eminent scholar Paul L. Maier has produced a modern translation of Josephus in his *Josephus: The Essential Writings*. For a study of how the events of 70 AD should influence New Testament interpretation, see *Before Jerusalem Fell* by Kenneth Gentry and *Biblical Hermeneutics* by Milton S. Terry. At a more popular level, David Chilton's *Paradise Restored* provides a helpful introduction.

160 **Wine with myrrh is a delicacy:** Pliny the Elder, *Natural History* 14.15: "The finest wine in early days was that spiced with the scent of myrrh."

160 **six feet from the stipes crucis:** Sanhedrin vi.3, 4.

CHAPTER 18

Iniuria: **The Injustice**

164 **hammer in hand, drives the spike into the wood:** If the spike is driven expertly, it does no injury to the artery nor does it fracture any of the delicate bones in the wrist. It does likely cut into the median nerve and it almost certainly impales the flexor pollicis longus. If so, Jesus immediately lost the use of his thumbs. The shooting pain would be horrific. (See Edwards, Gabel, and Hosmer, "Physical Death of Jesus Christ," 1459.)

165 **drives a spike through both feet:** The spike is driven "through the first or second intermetatarsal space, just distal to the tarsometatarsal joint. It is likely that the deep peroneal nerve and branches of the medial and lateral plantar nerves would have been injured." Ibid.; In 1968, an ossuary ("bone box") was found in Giv'at ha-Mivtar (ossuary no. 4 in Tomb 1). It contained the bones of a Jewish man named Yehohanan, who had been crucified during the time of Pontius Pilate. Apparently, the spike that pierced his feet could not be pulled out when he was taken down from his cross. It had apparently penetrated the heel bone (calcaneum) and deeply entered the wood. Those who took him down simply left the spike in his feet, and did not bother to remove the piece of olive wood that was attached to it. The ossuary, then, contained a heel bone pierced by an iron Roman

spike that was in turn embedded in a piece of wood. This is dramatic confirmation of how crucifixion was done in the time of Pilate and it supports the view of the gospel writers as to how Jesus Christ was crucified. For more on the Yohohanan remains, see Evans, *Jesus and His World*, 122–128.

167 *Father, forgive them:* Luke 23:34 (KJV).

168 *legionnaires call this "the dance of death":* This "dance of death" is why, when a victim lived too long and the Romans grew impatient, soldiers routinely broke the prisoner's legs. It was called the *crurifragium* and it prevented the condemned from pushing down on his feet in order to breathe. He quickly suffocated. This explains the events of John 19:32–33. Jesus was already dead and so his legs were not broken. The two criminals who were crucified with him were far from expired and so their legs were broken to hasten death because the Sabbath was approaching. Jewish law prevented leaving the bodies "on a tree" once the Sabbath had begun.

168 *let him save himself:* Luke 23:35.

168 *save yourself:* Luke 23:37.

168 *this man has done nothing wrong:* Luke 23:39–41.

168 *Jesus, remember me:* Luke 23:42.

169 *be with me in paradise:* Luke 23:43.

CHAPTER 19

Damnatus: **The Condemned**

173 *she told her children to rescue him:* Mark 3:21.

173 *sword will pierce your own soul:* Luke 2:35.

174 *here is your son:* John 19:26–27.

175 ***the world goes dark:*** In *The Day Christ Died* (p. 299), Jim Bishop has summarized the standard external evidence for this noon darkness: "The darkness, which was like looking through extra-strong sunglasses, seems to have pervaded the world at this hour. Phlegon wrote that in the fourth year of the two hundred and second Olympiad, there was a great darkness over Europe, surpassing anything that had ever been seen.

At midday, he said, the stars could be seen. At the same time an earthquake caused much damage in Nicaea. Tertullian said later that he found in the records of Rome a notation of worldwide darkness that the statesmen of the empire could not explain. Apparently the people of Jerusalem were accustomed to sudden changes in the weather, or there would have been a very wide sense of alarm or wonder at this time."

176 ***signal that God is moving:*** See Isaiah 13:9–10, Isaiah 34:4, Amos 8:9, and Ezekiel 32:7–8. A fine discussion of this symbolism is in *Biblical Hermeneutics* by Milton S. Terry.

178 ***As many as 150,000 people:*** Joachim Jeremias suggests the number of pilgrims at the feast in Jesus' day would have been 80,000–125,000, with an additional 30,000 permanent residents of Jerusalem in attendance also. This may be lessened by the fact that the poor were not required to provide lambs and some residents may have chosen not to participate. Still, the total would easily have been above 100,000. (Jeremias, *Eucharistic Words of Jesus*, 42.)

178 ***hours are rapidly approaching:*** Edersheim beautifully wrote, "The increasing, nameless agonies of the Crucifixion were deepening into the bitterness of death." (*Life and Times of Jesus*, 891.)

178 ***His heart is surrendering:*** Stated in more medical terms, the pericardium was filling with serum, compressing the heart.

178 ***Lamb of God, who takes away the sin:*** John 1:29, 35–36.

CHAPTER 20

Centurio: **The Centurion**

181 ***shouted out his last breath:*** There is something important happening here we shouldn't miss. N. T. Wright and Craig Evans explain this in their important little book, *Jesus, The Final Days*. They cite Mark 15:37(NRSV)—"Then Jesus gave a loud cry and breathed his last"— and then they write, "The act of shouting is itself the death. That is, Jesus does not shout out and then a moment later dies. His death manifests itself as a shout. By telling it this way, the evangelist Mark, if not the tradition before him, shows that Jesus' very death displays his power; the release of his spirit (as implied in the verb *exepneusen*) is awesome."

182 ***the man's death cry:*** Perhaps here is as good a place as any to ask the question, "What ultimately killed Jesus?" Here is the best summary for our purposes. It is from "On the Physical Death of Jesus Christ" by Edwards, Gabel, and Hosmer in the *Journal of the American Medical Association.*

"The fact that Jesus cried out in a loud voice and then bowed his head and died suggests the possibility of a catastrophic terminal event. One popular explanation has been that Jesus died of cardiac rupture. In the setting of the scourging and crucifixions with associated hypovolemia, hypoxemia, and perhaps an altered coagulable state, friable noninfective thrombotic vegetations could have formed on the aortic or mitral valve. These then could have dislodged and embolized into the coronary circulation and thereby produced an acute transmural myocardial infarction. Thrombotic valvular vegetations have been reported to develop under analogous acute traumatic conditions. Rupture of the left ventricular free wall may occur, though uncommonly, in the first few hours following infarction."

"However, another explanation may be more likely. Jesus' death may have been hastened simply by his state of exhaustion and by the severity of the scourging, with its resultant blood loss and preshock state. The fact that he could not carry his patibulum supports this interpretation. The actual cause of Jesus' death, like that of other crucified victims, may have been multifactorial and related primarily to hypovolemic shock, exhaustion asphyxia, and perhaps acute heart failure. A fatal cardiac arrhythmia may have accounted for the apparent catastrophic terminal event."

For further discussion and debate about the cause of death in crucifixion, see: Maslen and Mitchell, "Medical theories on the cause of death in crucifixion."

182 *the importance of what happened next:* Jim Bishop writes in his classic, *The Day Christ Died*, "The earth trembled and a small crack fissured the earth from the west toward the east and split the big rock of execution and went across the road and through the gate of Jerusalem and across the town and through the temple, and it split the big inner veil of the temple from the top to the bottom and went on east and rocked the big wall and split the tombs in the cemetery outside the walls and shook the Cedron and went on to the Dead Sea, leaving fissures in the earth, the rocks and across the mountains" (p. 308). There is little external evidence for this, but it does describe what most Christians believe and it is movingly written.

182 *the man's voice as he forced out his last words:* The four gospels list a number of wonders that occurred when Jesus surrendered his spirit at Golgotha. These include the earthquake, the rending of the temple curtain, the graves opening, and the dead rising. Some of these did not become public until after he rose from the dead. It is beyond the scope of this book to debate the historicity of these events, but it is helpful to note that Tacitus (*Histories* 5.13), Josephus (*Jewish Wars* 6.5.3), and even the Talmud (*Jer. Yoma* 43c; *Yoma* 39b) insist that a catastrophe occurred on the day Jesus Christ was cruci-

fied and that it was somehow related to the ultimate destruction of
the temple in 70 AD.

183 *centurion was changing religions:* Luke 23:47.

184 *given to whoever requests them for the purpose of burial:* Digesta
48.24.1.3

186 *blood and water pour out:* "The gospel of John describes the piercing of Jesus' side and emphasizes the sudden flow of blood and water.
Some authors have interpreted the flow of water to be ascites or urine,
from an abdominal midline perforation of the bladder. However, the
Greek word (πλευρα, or pleura) used by John clearly denoted later-
ality and often implied the ribs. Therefore, it seems probable that the
wound was in the thorax and well away from the abdominal midline." See Edwards, Gabel, and Hosmer, "On the Physical Death of
Jesus Christ," 1462.

186 *John, Jesus' friend, sees this:* The apostle John writes of this in his
gospel: "These things happened so that the scripture would be ful-
filled: 'Not one of his bones will be broken,' and, as another scripture
says, 'They will look on the one they have pierced'" (John 19:36–
37). Clearly, by quoting Exodus 12:46, John is affirming that Jesus is
the sacrificial lamb of the Passover.

187 *the centurion "praised God":* Luke 23:47.

CHAPTER 21

Excessum: **The Departure**

191 *going "boldly" to Pilate:* Mark 15:43.

192 *Nicodemus joins him:* It is intriguing that Nicodemus may be mentioned in rabbinic sources. A Nicodemus, son of Gorion, is mentioned as a wealthy man and a member of the council. During the

siege that ended in 70 AD, one of Nicodemus' granaries in Galilee burned down. He likely died during this time. His daughter later died in poverty. (*Encyclopedia Judaica* 12 [Jerusalem: Encyclopedia Judaica, 1971], 801–802; Flusser and Notley, *The Sage from Galilee*, 140–41).

193   *a handful of faithful women:* Mark 15:40–41.

Epilogue

200   ***doing something interesting with food:*** Mark 16:14; Luke 24:41–42; John 21.

202   ***two men walking down a road:*** The story that follows is from Luke 24:13–35.

206   ***his disciples did not abandon him:*** Maier, *Josephus: The Essential Writings*, 265. This famous quote from Josephus, called the *Testimonium Flavianum*, has been challenged by some scholars who believe it is too "Christian" for Josephus and that someone devoted to Jesus probably inserted it long after Josephus lived. However, in 1972, Professor Schlomo Pines of the Hebrew University in Jerusalem announced that he had discovered an Arabic manuscript by the Melkite Agapius of the tenth century and that this passage from Josephus was included, though in a more Jewish mode of expression. It aligned closely with the "Christian" version some scholars had rejected. Pines concluded that the above text must have been in Josephus' original and this is now the standard view. See Pines, *An Arabic Version of the Testimonium Flavianum*.

Ancient Authors on the Death of Jesus

208 *there was about this time Jesus, a wise man:* William Whiston, trans., *The Works of Josephus*, (Peabody, MA: Hendrickson Publishers, 1987). On the accuracy of the *Testimonium Flavianum:* See Maier, *Josephus: The Essential Writings*, 265. This famous quote from Josephus, called the *Testimonium Flavianum*, has been challenged by some scholars who believe it is too "Christian" for Josephus and that someone devoted to Jesus probably inserted it long after Josephus lived. However, in 1972, Professor Schlomo Pines of the Hebrew University in Jerusalem announced that he had discovered an Arabic manuscript by the Melkite Agapius of the tenth century and that this passage from Josephus was included, though in a more Semitic mode of expression. It aligned closely with the "Christian" version some scholars had rejected. Pines concluded that the above text must have been in Josephus' original and this is now the standard view. See Pines, *An Arabic Version*.

BIBLIOGRAPHY

Bauckham, Richard. *Jesus and the Eyewitnesses*. Grand Rapids: Wm. B. Eerdmans, 2006.

Barbet, Pierre. *A Doctor at Calvary: The Passion of Our Lord Jesus Christ as Described by a Surgeon*. Fort Collins: Roman Catholic Books, 1953.

Bishop, Jim. *The Day Christ Died*. New York: Harper & Brothers, 1957.

————. *The Day Christ Was Born*. New York: Harper & Brothers, 1959.

Bock, Darrell L., and Gregory J. Herrick. *Jesus in Context*. Grand Rapids: Baker Academic, 2005.

Borg, Marcus, and John Dominic Crossan. *The Last Week: A Day-by-Day Account of Jesus's Final Week in Jerusalem*. New York: HarperCollins, 2006.

Brandon, S. G. F. *The Trial of Jesus of Nazareth*. New York: Dorset, 1968.

Brodrick, M. *The Trial and Crucifixion of Jesus of Nazareth*. London: J. Murray, 1908.

Bruce, F. F. *The New Testament Documents: Are They Reliable?* Blacksburg: Wilder Publications, 2009.

Cahill, Thomas. *Desire of the Everlasting Hills: The World Before and After Jesus*. New York: Anchor Books, 1999.

————. *The Gifts of the Jews: How a Tribe of Nomads Changed the Way Everyone Thinks and Feels*. New York: Anchor Books, 1998.

Carcopino, Jerome. *Daily Life in Ancient Rome*. Edited by Henry T. Rowell. Translated by E. O. Lorimer. New Haven: Yale University Press, 1968.

Chandler, William M. *The Trial of Jesus from a Lawyer's Standpoint*. New York: Empire, 1908.

Chapman, David W. *Ancient Jewish and Christian Perceptions of Crucifixion*. Grand Rapids: Baker Academic, 2008.

Charlesworth, James H., ed. *Jesus and Archaeology*. Grand Rapids: Wm. B. Eerdmans, 2006.

Church, Alfred John, and William Jackson Brodribb, trans. *The Complete Works of Tacitus*. New York: Modern Library, 1942.

Coulter, Fred R. *The Day Christ Died*. Hollister: York, 2004.

Danby, Herbert, trans. *The Mishnah*. New York: Oxford University Press, 1933.

Davie, John, trans. Seneca: *Dialogues and Essays*. New York: Oxford University Press, 2007.

Edersheim, Alfred. *The Life and Times of Jesus the Messiah*. Peabody, MA: Hendrickson, 1993.

————. *Sketches of Jewish Social Life*. Peabody, MA: Hendrickson, 1994.

————. *The Temple: Its Ministry and Services*. Peabody, MA: Hendrickson, 1994.

Edwards, William D., Wesley J. Gabel, and Floyd E. Hosmer. "On the Physical Death of Jesus Christ." *Journal of the American Medical Association* 255, no. 11 (March 21, 1986): 1455–1463.

Evans, Craig A. *Jesus and His World: The Archaeological Evidence*. Louisville: Westminster John Knox Press, 2012.

————. *Jesus and the Ossuaries*. Waco, TX: Baylor University Press, 2003.

Evans, Craig A., and N. T. Wright. *Jesus, The Final Days: What Really Happened*. Louisville: Westminster John Knox Press, 2009.

Farrar, Frederick William. *The Life of Christ*. Whitefish, MT: Kessinger, 2010.

Feldman, Louis H. *Jew and Gentile in the Ancient World*. Princeton: Princeton University Press, 1993.

Flusser, David, with R. Steven Notley. *The Sage from Galilee: Rediscovering Jesus' Genius*. Grand Rapids: Wm. B. Eerdmans, 2007.

Fox, Robin Lane. *Pagans and Christians*. New York: Alfred A. Knopf, 1987.

Frazee, Charles A. *Two Thousand Years Ago: The World at the Time of Jesus*. Grand Rapids: Wm. B. Eerdmans, 2002.

Hamilton, Edith. *The Greek Way*. New York: W. W. Norton, 1964.

Hengel, Martin. *Crucifixion in the Ancient World and the Folly of the Message of the Cross*. Philadelphia: Fortress Press, 1977.

Hill, Daniel. *The Crucifixion of Christ*. Philadelphia: William S. & Alfred Martien, 1859.

Jeremias, Joachim. *Jerusalem in the Time of Jesus*. Philadelphia: Fortress Press, 1969.

————. *The Eucharistic Words of Jesus*. Norwich, UK: SCM Press, 1977.

Jones, C. David. *The Apostles of Jesus Christ*. Fort Wayne: Phalanx Associates, 2001.

Jowett, Benjamin, trans. *Plato's Republic*. Millis, MA: Agora, 2001.

Lewis, E. G. *At Table with the Lord*. North Bend, OR: Cape Arago Press, 2010.

Louth, Andrew, ed. *Early Christian Writings: The Apostolic Fathers*. New York: Penguin Books, 1968.

Maier, Paul. trans. *Josephus: The Essential Writings*. Grand Rapids: Kregel, 1988.

Marinella, Mark A. *Died He for Me*. Ventura, CA: Nordskog, 2008.

Maslen, Matthew W., and Piers D. Mitchell. "Medical Theories on the Cause of Death in Crucifixion." *Journal of the Royal Society of Medicine* 99 (2006): 185.

McDowell, Josh, and Bill Wilson. *The Evidence for the Historical Jesus*. Eugene, OR: Harvest House, 1988.

Morris, Leon. *The Cross in the New Testament*. Grand Rapids: Wm. B. Eerdmans, 1965.

————. *The Gospel according to John*. Grand Rapids: Wm. B. Eerdmans, 1995.

Page, Nick. *The Longest Week*. London: Hodder & Stoughton, 2009.

Pines, Schlomo. *An Arabic Version of the Testimonium Flavianum and Its Implications*. Jerusalem: Israel Academy of Sciences and Humanities, 1971.

Pollard, Nigel. *Soldiers, Cities, and Civilians in Roman Syria*. Ann Arbor: University of Michigan Press, 2000.

Powell, Frank J. *The Trial of Jesus Christ*. Grand Rapids: Wm. B. Eerdmans, 1949.

Reader, John. *Cities*. London: Heinemann, 2004.

Reinhartz, Adele. *Caiaphas the High Priest.* Studies on Personalities of the New Testament, edited by Moody D. Smith. Minneapolis: Fortress Press, 2013.

Richardson, Peter. *Building Jewish in the Roman East.* Waco, TX: Baylor University Press, 2004.

Sakenfeld, Katherine Doob, Samuel E. Balentine et al, eds. *The New Interpreter's Dictionary of the Bible.* Nashville: Abingdon Press, 2006.

Sanders, E. P. *The Historical Figure of Jesus.* London: Penguin, 1995.

Tenney, Merrill C. *New Testament Survey.* Grand Rapids: Eerdmans, 1985.

Terry, Milton S. *Biblical Hermeneutics.* Grand Rapids: Academie Books, 1989.

Unger, Merrill F. *Archaeology and the New Testament.* Grand Rapids: Zondervan, 1962.

Vardaman, E. Jerry, ed. *Chronos, Kairos, Christos II: Chronological, Nativity, and Religious Studies in Memory of Ray Summers.* Macon, GA: Mercer University Press, 1998.

Walker, Peter. *The Weekend That Changed the World.* Louisville: Westminster John Knox Press, 1999.

Whiston, William, trans. *The Works of Josephus.* Peabody, MA: Hendrickson, 1987.

Wilken, Robert Louis. *The Christians As the Romans Saw Them.* New Haven: Yale University Press, 1984.

Zugibe, Frederick T. *The Crucifixion of Jesus: A Forensic Inquiry.* New York: M. Evans, 2005.

ACKNOWLEDGMENTS

My life has been defined by friendships. Some were seasonal. Some were conducted over great distances. Some faded and then returned. Some were deep and then were lost forever. All have left a mark. My life has been defined by friendships. It is a profound gift, and it has shaped nearly every word upon these pages.

In the months it took to write this book, I followed Jesus from his triumphal entry into Jerusalem to his brutal death. As I did, I remembered that Wayne Palmer and Dr. Howard M. Ervin were the first to describe to me the horrors of that death. I recalled, too, that scholars like Dr. Jerry Horner and Dr. Auden Autry taught me about the world in which that death occurred. Life-changing books—also the gifts of friends—played a role, and these included Jim Bishop's *The Day Christ Died, Josephus: The Essential Writings* by Paul Maier, Alfred Edersheim's *The Life and Times of Jesus the Messiah*, and *A Doctor at Calvary* by Pierre Barbet. Then there were the mystics who fearlessly lived the meaning of Christ crucified before me—Dr. Robert Stamps,

John Michael Talbot, and Richard Glickstein—as well as the pastors who worked to imbed this meaning in my life: Brett Fuller, Father Thomas McKenzie, Jim Critcher, and Jim Laffoon. How could I be anything but grateful?

I felt the imprint of friends every day I wrote. The accomplished actor Chip Arnold advised me on the shape of the narrative. Eminent Anglican scholar N. T. Wright guided me through difficult New Testament passages. Friend and Fulbright scholar Adam Claasen of Massey University in New Zealand expertly recommended sources. Dr. George Grant—always encouraging, always on my side, always in the grand tradition of Reformed scholarship, and always hungry for barbecue—kept me on track theologically and corrected my pitiful Latin. Professor Ben Crist helped us both—*gratias tibi ago*. Morris Proctor, owner and developer of systems like Libronix, served as mentor in the technology of my work.

When I traveled to Israel to walk the soil beneath this story, Dr. Rice Broocks activated his network there. I was well tended. Samuel Smadja of Sar-El Tours and his amazing scholar/guide, Rodney Gilla, provided an entire graduate education in just a few days. Wayne and Ann Hillsden became new friends as they taught me from their decades in the land. Ron Cantor made me laugh and question when I so desperately wanted to sleep. I'm grateful for them all.

It was wisely said that a man's critics are the unpaid guardians of his soul. The same is true of scholarship. Those who approach facts from a different vantage point serve us best in our efforts to arrive at truth. They probe, challenge, defy, defend, and accuse. It forces us to improve. Several editors who cannot be named served me in this way. Their benign disagreement and disarming grace changed both this book and its author.

Worthy Publishing was a fine partner in this venture. I'm grateful for the opportunity to work with them on a story of this import and grateful, too, for their devotion to telling the story well. They brought me into contact with Marcus Brotherton, who graced this project with both his excellence and editorial skill. Immensely helpful also were Kyle Olund, Melissa Campbell-Goodson, Dr. Mark Wilson, Dan Posthuma, Father Thomas McKenzie, Lynn Green, and Dan Williamson. Their insights encouraged, corrected, and inspired.

Always with me was Chartwell Literary Group, and I could not have pulled this off without them. A book of this kind can be excruciatingly difficult to edit and organize. It employs four languages, three dating systems, a dozen narrative perspectives, and then it attempts to popularize a complex, controversial story that took place twenty centuries ago. Undaunted, Chartwell skillfully sharpened the manuscript, kept me in harmony with the fine folks at Worthy Publishing, and parked the manuscript on time with its author still emitting vital signs. They are a miracle.

Given my decision to write largely in public places, I must thank T. J. Stone's Grill House and Tap Room, Bruegger's Bagels, The Torpedo Factory, the Fairfax County Sheriff's Office, and Huntley Meadows Park—all in Alexandria, Virginia. Helpful, too, were the artisans remodeling my beloved Union Station, the Delta Airlines ground crew at Ronald Reagan Washington National Airport, and the staff at Arlington National Cemetery in Washington, DC. My gratitude, also, to the many strangers who kindly played a role, particularly in Israel.

Finally, the devotion of my life to Beverly, who endured all and loves me still. This too is a miracle, as is all we have found together in the second act of our days in this world. *Praestat sero quam nunquam.**

---

* *"Better late than never."*

ABOUT THE AUTHOR

Stephen Mansfield is the *New York Times* best-selling author of books on faith, history, and contemporary culture. His works include *The Faith of George W. Bush*, *The Search for God and Guinness*, *The Faith of Barack Obama*, and *Lincoln's Battle with God*. He is a popular speaker and a commentator for several major news networks. Mansfield lives in Nashville and Washington, DC, with his wife, Beverly, who is an award-winning songwriter and producer. (MansfieldGroup.com)

WORTHY
PUBLISHING

IF YOU ENJOYED THIS BOOK, WILL YOU CONSIDER SHARING THE MESSAGE WITH OTHERS?

- Mention the book in a Facebook post, Twitter update, Pinterest pin, or blog post.

- Recommend this book to those in your small group, book club, workplace, and classes.

- Head over to facebook.com/mansfieldwrites, "LIKE" the page, and post a comment as to what you enjoyed the most.

- Tweet "I recommend reading #KillingJesus by @MansfieldWrites // @worthypub"

- Pick up a copy for someone you know who would be challenged and encouraged by this message.

- Write a review on amazon.com, bn.com, goodreads.com, or cbd.com.

You can subscribe to Worthy Publishing's newsletter at worthypublishing.com.

**WORTHY PUBLISHING
FACEBOOK PAGE**

**WORTHY PUBLISHING
WEBSITE**